"Dan and Ed have extracted great Christian living lessons from baseball. The pages of *The Winning Run* crackle with informative and entertaining insights."

—ERNIE HARWELL, baseball announcer

"With every game I play I become more convinced that baseball simply mirrors the world we live in. Dan and Ed have done a great job of drawing attention to what I feel is the real value of baseball: using it as a tool to teach life's lessons."

—TRAVIS FRYMAN, major league veteran
and all-star husband and father

THE
WINNING RUN

and Other
LifeLessons
from
Baseball

Dan Bolin
and
Ed Diaz

NAVPRESS⬤
BRINGING TRUTH TO LIFE
P.O. Box 35001, Colorado Springs, Colorado 80935

OUR GUARANTEE TO YOU

We believe so strongly in the message of our books that we are making this quality guarantee to you. If for any reason you are disappointed with the content of this book, return the title page to us with your name and address and we will refund to you the list price of the book. To help us serve you better, please briefly describe why you were disappointed. Mail your refund request to: NavPress, P.O. Box 35002, Colorado Springs, CO 80935.

The Navigators is an international Christian organization. Our mission is to reach, disciple, and equip people to know Christ and to make Him known through successive generations. We envision multitudes of diverse people in the United States and every other nation who have a passionate love for Christ, live a lifestyle of sharing Christ's love, and multiply spiritual laborers among those without Christ.

NavPress is the publishing ministry of The Navigators. NavPress publications help believers learn biblical truth and apply what they learn to their lives and ministries. Our mission is to stimulate spiritual formation among our readers.

Cover design by Dan Jamison
Cover illustration by Frank Hoffman / Wood River Media, Inc.

Some of the anecdotal illustrations in this book are true to life and are included with the permission of the persons involved. All other illustrations are composites of real situations, and any resemblance to people living or dead is coincidental.

Scripture quotations in this publication are taken from the *HOLY BIBLE: NEW INTERNATIONAL VERSION* ® (NIV®). Copyright © 1973, 1978, 1984 by International Bible Society. Used by permission of Zondervan Publishing House. All rights reserved. Other versions used include: the *New American Standard Bible* (NASB), © The Lockman Foundation 1960, 1962, 1963, 1968, 1971, 1972, 1973, 1975, 1977; and the *King James Version* (KJV).

Printed in the United States of America

1 2 3 4 5 6 7 8 9 10 11 12 13 14 15 / 05 04 03 02 01 00 99

FOR A FREE CATALOG OF
NAVPRESS BOOKS & BIBLE STUDIES,
CALL 1-800-366-7788 (USA)
OR 1-416-499-4615 (CANADA)

To Haley Bolin,
my beloved daughter,
in whom I am well pleased.

—DAN BOLIN

To Zach, MattE, Ben, and Jonathan, my sons,
who have taught me far more about
God's love than I have taught
them about baseball.

—ED DIAZ

CONTENTS

Preface

Quick, who won the 1991 World Series?

Not that long ago was it? But since then other World Series have come and gone. Sports seasons have run their cycles and life has a way of filling each moment with its immediate cares and concerns. But in October 1991 you would have known the winner as well as you knew your birthday. Yes, life has a way of covering over the things that once were central to our attention.

This can happen in our spiritual lives as well. Those concerns and disciplines that we held close to our hearts can drift away unless we attend to them on a regular basis. We'll quickly lose our spiritual intensity and commitment if we allow the steady stream of distractions to control our lives.

We must find a way to bring our attention back to the things of God in order to maintain and develop our spiritual fire. In *Mere Christianity,* C. S. Lewis is speaking about faith when he says, "If you have once accepted Christianity, then some of its main doctrines shall be deliberately held before your mind for some time every day. That is why daily prayers and religious reading and church going are necessary parts of the Christian life. We have to be continually reminded of what we believe. Neither this belief nor any other will automatically remain alive in the mind. It must be fed."

This book is about not drifting away from God. It's about anchoring ourselves deeply in a love relationship with God. Not a mushy love, based on our emotions only, but a love that involves our heart, soul, mind, and strength.

This book is targeted toward men. The pressures of life and the intense time demands can quickly drain the spiritual life from a man's heart of hearts. I hope females will read and profit from these thoughts—but it is a book directed toward men.

Any project like this involves the help of many gifted people. Cay Bolin and Gwen Diaz are at the top of the list. Zach, MattE, Ben, and Jonathan Diaz provided their input, as did Haley Bolin. Sue Geiman, Steve Webb, and Gary Wilde gave significantly along the way.

And by the way, the Twins won the 1991 World Series.

DAN BOLIN
November 1998

INTRODUCTION

One of my favorite movie lines comes from *A League of Their Own*. A hung-over Jimmy Dugan (played by Tom Hanks) attempts to manage his first professional baseball team, an all-women's team. Near the beginning of their first game, Dugan screams at one of his outfielders who has just missed her cut-off man. When she dissolves into tears, Dugan exclaims in disbelief from the dugout, "There is no crying in baseball!"

While that quote has become famous, I know for a fact that it's not true. Jimmy Dugan obviously never witnessed my very first at bat in a Little League game. I was a chubby, hesitant eight-year-old facing a much older pitcher who was throwing sidearm. When his first pitch landed squarely in the middle of my back, I learned—without a doubt—there *is* crying in baseball.

Though not every line in *A League of Their Own* is totally accurate, there is a great scene near the end of the movie that attempts to summarize all of life. Dottie Hinson (played by Geena Davis) has decided to leave the team and return to Oregon with her husband, just before the first All-American Women's Professional Baseball League World Series. As Coach Dugan discovers that his best player is about to leave, he approaches her car and queries, "Taking a little day trip?"

"No, Bob and I are driving home—to Oregon," Dottie replies.

"You know, I really thought you were a ballplayer," Dugan comments, obviously trying to kindle her competitive spirit.

"Well, you were wrong," Dottie responds quietly.

"Was I?"

Dottie doesn't budge. "Yeah, it's only a game, Jimmy, and I don't need this. I have Bob. I don't need this. I don't."

After a little more conversation, Dugan pointedly challenges her. "I'm in no position to tell anyone how to live, but sneaking out like this—quitting—you'll regret it for the rest of your life. Baseball is what gets inside you. It's what lights you up. You can't *deny* that."

"It's just too hard," Dottie responds tearfully.

(Don't miss this. Here's the great line . . .)

"It's *supposed* to be hard." Dugan is animated and adamant. "If it wasn't hard, everyone would do it! The *hard* is what makes it *great!*"

Indeed, "the hard" is what makes baseball great. No other sports season is played out like a marathon with such a myriad of ups and downs. Perhaps no other sport mirrors the Christian life so well—a myriad of ups and downs played out over the marathon of one's life.

But it is "the hard" that makes the Christian life so great. Jesus Christ Himself understood this. His hardest struggle of all became our greatest triumph. His "hard" made life "great" for us. His death on the cross made it possible for us to have eternal life.

Our focus in this book is to learn about life as we observe the game of baseball. It's to take lessons from the dugout to our dining rooms, from the on-deck circle to our offices, from the field to our families. Both at home and on the baseball field, our response to all of life's ups and downs should be to imitate Christ as He faced the challenges of life.

> *[He] committed no sin, nor was any deceit found in His mouth; and while being reviled, He did not revile in return; while suffering, He uttered no threats, but kept entrusting Himself to Him who judges right-eously; and He Himself bore our sins in His body on the cross, that we might die to sin and live to right-eousness; for by His wounds you were healed.* (1 Peter 2:22-24)

There is crying in life as there is in baseball. But it's "the HARD" that makes it possible to enjoy "the GREAT"!

ED DIAZ

Note to the Reader:
You can use this book in a variety of ways. Of course, you might choose to read a chapter a day for a month. Great! But don't limit yourself to that kind of rigorous reading plan if your schedule would tend to make it a chore. In that case, try these options:

- Read a chapter a week for thirty-one weeks, perhaps on a Saturday night before Sunday worship;

- Read chapters with a group of friends and discuss your reactions and insights together—whenever you can meet;

- Read every time you watch a ball game, or whenever you *think* about watching or playing baseball;

- Or just read when the Spirit moves you.

Reading this book ought to be like taking a breath of fresh air whenever you need it. So no matter how you plan your devotional times, let them become quality visits with the Lord. Invite His presence as you read, pray, and meditate upon what He has to say to your heart. That way, you'll be launching into the deeper waters of faith—with Him by your side.

ONE

SAFE AT HOME

EVERY BATTER WHO STEPS UP TO THE PLATE HAS ONE GOAL IN MIND: He wants to go home. However, he'll have to touch four bases to arrive safely at his destination.

Have you noticed a parallel in the Christian life? Every believer in Christ who leaves this earth is headed for heaven, "going home." But in this case, too, four bases come first. Let's consider them for a moment.

First Base: God's Position

The one who wants to make it home with the Lord must recognize some things about Him. First, God loves us. John 3:16 tells us, *God so loved the world that he gave his only begotten Son.* However, God is not only a loving God, He is absolutely perfect. In Matthew 5:48 Jesus says,

> *Therefore you are to be perfect, as your heavenly Father is perfect.*

God's position—right there at first base—is one of love and perfection. Don't miss that!

Second Base: Our Position

The Bible describes our condition before God in two ways.

17

First, we are not perfect. According to Romans 3:23, we've all sinned and fallen short of God's perfection. The result is that we are separated from God. Romans 6:23 says,

The wages of sin is death.

Second, just as physical death means separation from our physical bodies, spiritual death means separation from the source of all spiritual life. Because of our sin we cannot enter God's holy, perfect presence.

Smead Jolley was a great major league hitter, but he had a terrible time playing the field. One afternoon, Smead was playing left field, seemingly the safest place to hide his defensive liabilities. Sure enough, a line drive headed his way and rolled between his legs. Jolley raced back. The ball bounced off the wall right at him—and rolled between his legs again! He finally chased the ball down, but by then the runner was headed for third. Smead threw the ball, but it sailed into the stands, allowing the batter to score. Jolley set a record for three errors on one play.

Although we normally don't make three errors on one play, we are by no means perfect. Just as every major league player is charged with an error at some time during his career, there isn't a single one of us without an "E" by his name in the stat book of life.

Third Base: God's Provision
The great message of Christianity is that although we are sinful and separated from God, He provided a way for us to enter His holy presence. God sent a substitute who was willing to suffer

the consequences of our imperfection. That substitute is Jesus Christ. Romans 5:8 tells us,

> *But God demonstrates His own love toward us, in that while we were yet sinners, Christ died for us.*

Jesus Christ is our pinch hitter, our pinch runner, and our perfect substitute in the game of life. He makes up for all of our errors by being our sacrifice. He died on the cross so that we don't have to experience the punishment of eternal separation from God, which we deserve. All of our "Es" are wiped out of the record book.

Going Home: Our Decision

God's only requirement is that we *believe* in order to be pronounced "safe" when we touch "home plate." John 3:16 concludes *that whoever believes in Him should not perish, but have eternal life.*

Three Latin words can translate our one English word "believe." The first is *noticea* (to notice), which means to acquire an intellectual knowledge of something. The second, *assencia* (to assent), means to agree with a set of facts. Both of these are good words, but neither of them is the biblical word used in John 3:16. The word for "believe" in this passage is the Latin word *fiducia*. It means to entrust one's life to another person, allowing him to do what he promised he would do.

Fiducia takes place every time a major league team flies to a new city. It is not enough for them to *noticea* or *assencia* that airplanes can fly. Players might be tempted merely to study aerodynamics or interview the pilots. No, they cannot fly to an out-of-town series unless they are willing to *step aboard the airplane.*

Our relationship with God through Christ begins that way. It is not enough to notice that Jesus Christ lived two thousand years ago or to accept the facts about His life. We must, in a sense, "step on board" and trust Him to do what He promised He would do—wipe out our errors and grant us eternal life.

ED DIAZ

EXTRA INNINGS
READ 1 PETER 3:15

- Which Latin word, *noticea*, *assencia*, or *fiducia*, best describes your belief in God? How can you be sure you're going to be "safe" at home plate?
- Do you have friends who might not be "safe" when they reach home plate because they have not believed using the *fiducia* definition? Are you willing and able to explain your faith to them?

T W O

Spurred to Third

Before Haley started school, she was playing third base in T-ball. The fact that she and the other five- and six-year-olds barely knew the way to first base didn't dampen their enthusiasm. The kids enjoyed the games and the parents loved to see the future Hall-of-Famers learn the basics. The fielding was always atrocious so there was an adventure every time the ball was put into play. Fortunately, there was a six run limit each inning and the strategy was to keep running.

Haley could field, throw, and hit about as well as the others but she distinguished herself running the bases. One afternoon her bat did meet the ball and it sailed into left field. Haley rounded first and dug for second. Then the third base coach decided to get aggressive and waved her on to third. He knew she was fast, and no one expected an accurate throw from a player exiled to the outfield.

But this time the throw was on the money; Haley was out at third.

To Whom Are You Listening?
The tears rolled and it seemed as though the end of her life was at hand. No one felt worse than the third base coach, except maybe Haley. Generally, the base coach can see what

is happening in the field much better than the runner, who's too busy making progress to watch the action behind him. It's wonderful to have help making tough decisions on the fly.

As we round the base paths of life, we encounter many people ready to give us advice. Some know what they're talking about and some don't. Consider the case of Rehoboam, for instance, the newly appointed king of Israel. His father, Solomon, had been the wisest man ever, and that provided him quite a legacy to live up to.

His first challenge was taxation. Solomon had built the infrastructure of the nation, adding the temple, his palace, a huge army, cities, a fleet—not to mention the thousand wives he supported. This cost the nation dearly, and the people came to the new king asking for a tax rollback. In 1 Kings 12:4 they say,

> *Your father put a heavy yoke on us, but lighten the harsh labor and the heavy yoke he put on us and we will serve you.*

What's a young king to do? His first instinct was his best. He asked the men who had served his father in court. These men had grappled with issues of state their whole lives, and they'd been trained by Solomon to deal with these issues. They gave him good advice:

> *If today you will be a servant to these people and serve them and give them a favorable answer, they will always be your servants.* (verse 7)

Sage advice from seasoned veterans. These wise men understood the moment and the long-term implications for the young king's reign.

But Rehoboam rejected the advice the elders gave him and consulted the young men that he had grown up with. (verse 8)

The advice of Rehoboam's childhood friends, though, was to get tough with the people, show them who was boss, and demand even more from them. And that's exactly what he did.

Rehoboam's actions sent the nation into civil war, with the king himself barely escaping with his life. His nation went to pieces within the first few days of his reign. Ten of the twelve tribes revolted, leaving Rehoboam with a fraction of the nation he could have ruled if he had followed good advice.

It's Your Call!
Who we listen to is critical. We need godly advisers around us who can keep us from making huge mistakes with dire consequences. Do you have a group of friends who can evaluate your situation honestly and love you enough to tell you the truth?

DAN BOLIN

EXTRA INNINGS
READ PROVERBS 8:10-14

- What three things are considered more valuable than precious metals and jewels?
- Who is the source of sound judgment? How do you tap into that wisdom in daily life?

THREE

Chapel Service

I'VE BEEN PRIVILEGED TO SPEAK AT A FEW TEXAS RANGERS chapel services before home games on Sundays. The visiting team holds a separate chapel, as well, and I enjoy meeting the players and sharing some thoughts from Scripture with them.

One Sunday about twenty players from the visiting team gathered in the exercise room to hear my words of encouragement. John Weber, the Rangers' chaplain, introduced me to the team. He said nice things about my family and me and told them I was the director of a Christian summer camp. Then John asked, "How many of you attended summer camp when you were kids?" Most of those at chapel had been raised in Latin America where Christian camping isn't well established yet. No one raised his hand, and by the blank stares I could tell most didn't have a clue as to what John was talking about.

Then John tried to think of the institution that most resembled a Christian camp and asked, "Well, how many of you were in juvenile detention homes growing up?" To our surprise, six honest hands went up. And then a voice at the back said, "But sir, I've been clean and sober for over six years!"

In the Renewal Business
There was a good laugh all around, and I doubt if any of those

24

players have a clue to this day as to the meaning of "Christian camp." The thing I took with me is the strength and sincere pride of the young ballplayer who had been able to face his problems and overcome them. For six years he had lived free of the sin that had entrapped him, fighting day by day to stay clean and sober.

God is in the business of renewing lives that have been hammered by sinful behavior, and He does it through pure grace. David understood God's grace in a very personal and powerful way when he wrote Psalm 51, having been over-whelmed with the extent of his own sinful transgressions. Four key verses in this psalm of repentance show how graciously God restores us.

Verse 1 states,

Have mercy on me, O God, according to your unfailing love; according to your great compassion blot out my transgressions.

All forgiveness of sin is based upon God's character and His desire to reveal His unfailing love and boundless compassion. When we sin and need mercy, it is totally a "God issue." He shows us mercy because of who He is, not because of what we deserve.

Verses 4 begins,

Against you, you only, have I sinned.

We may hurt others by our wrongdoings, but acts of sin are, in essence, a direct rebellion against God Himself. In doing them, we're saying we know better than God what is best for our lives. We usurp His position of sovereignty and put our own desires on the throne. Our sin is a *coup d'état* against the Ruler of the universe, and it is doomed to failure from the start.

Verse 10 says,

Create in me a pure heart, O God, and renew a steadfast spirit within me.

When we come to the point of recognizing the folly of our attempts to bring peace and fulfillment to our lives through independent acts of rebellion, we're ready for something new and better. God wants us to have a pure, clean heart focused on Him. He wants a steadfast spirit to rule our thoughts and actions so we can hear and obey His directives for our lives.

Verse 17 states,

The sacrifices of God are a broken spirit; a broken and contrite heart, O God, you will not despise.

Broken spirits and broken hearts are what God is eager to comfort and use. Our throwaway society sees broken items as having lost their usefulness. But from God's perspective, broken spirits and broken hearts are ready for His comforting response, and they are ready for Him to use.

Until we come to the end of our rope we may not appreciate the depth of God's comfort or the love He extends to us in our unworthiness. Perhaps we expect that He'll despise us for our weakness and sinful condition, but just the opposite is true. Our brokenness and admission of need makes us a perfect target for God's love and care.

That clean-and-sober young ballplayer had struggled each

day as he fought to overcome the patterns of his sinful past. And I'm sure he still faces daily battles with temptation, just as we all do. But God sees our broken spirits and He holds our contrite hearts in His hands. Remaking and strengthening hearts is God's specialty. Let Him provide His healing touch for you.

DAN BOLIN

EXTRA INNINGS
READ PSALM 23

- Think of the things a shepherd does for his sheep. What is David saying about God's relationship to us?
- What does "He restores my soul" in verse 3 mean to you? Does your soul need some restoration today? What is the first step to take toward that end?

ERNIE HARWELL

I GREW UP IN THE MOUNTAINS OF NORTHEASTERN PENNSYL-vania—equidistant between the major sports cities of New York and Philadelphia. Because of the influence of my Uncle "Snuffy" who raised me, I was a committed Yankee fan throughout my entire childhood. Because we could listen to each and every Yankees telecast, "Baseball and Ballantine" was so ingrained in my psyche that I didn't realize one word could be used without the other. Mel Allen, the "Voice of the Yankees," was a part of my life from birth until age eighteen—when I left for college in . . . Philadelphia!

During the following transitory years, I tried to maintain a rooting interest in the teams of the various cities where I lived. As I made my home in Philadelphia, Dallas, Portland, and Atlanta, I resolved to cheer for the Phillies, Rangers, Mariners, and Braves. But alas—no team ever appealed to me as did the Yankees of my youth.

That is, until Ernie Harwell entered my life.

Listening to the Old Master
Ernie is the Hall of Fame announcer for the Detroit Tigers. I had never been a Tiger fan, but in 1983 my family and I moved to Lakeland, Florida, the spring training home of the Detroit ball

club. Soon after, I was invited to teach a couples' Bible study with the major leaguers and arrange for chapel each Sunday. As my involvement with Baseball Chapel grew, so did my relationship with Mr. Harwell. Unfortunately, once spring training ended, the Tigers always went north, and few television broadcasts of their games were available. Consequently, I found myself listening to radio play-by-play done by the old master Harwell himself.

What a joy to listen to Ernie paint a picture of Tiger Stadium and the events taking place at the corner of Michigan and Trumble! Although I had never been to Tiger Stadium I could visualize every pitch. Every home run was "loooooong gone," and every called third strike found the surprised hitter "standing there like the house beside the road." The "emerald grass of the outfield" was surrounded by the "ocean blue of the grandstands."

I soon became a loyal fan.

On one pleasant occasion I was invited to accompany the Tigers on a road trip. Because my schedule was wide open, I had little to do at game time except sit alone with fans of the opposing team. All that changed, however, when Ernie asked if I would like to visit him in the broadcast booth. *Would I?* I could think of nothing more fascinating than to sit through a radio broadcast next to Ernie Harwell. So the details were arranged. I was to accompany Ernie to the booth and watch him at his artistic best.

As the game commenced, an eerie nostalgia came over me, a reminiscence of those days back in the mountains of Pennsylvania when I sat glued to the radio listening to Mel

Allen—except that, in front of me on the field below, the real game was being played. Hearing Ernie, seated on my left, describing each event as it actually unfolded before me on the playing field is one of the highlights of my love affair with baseball.

Moving into the Booth

As I ponder this incredible opportunity, I am reminded of Hebrews 11:1:

> *Now faith is the assurance of things hoped for, the conviction of things not seen.*

The word *assurance* has a wonderful meaning. It can be translated literally as "title deed."

I drive a 1992 Chevy van. It's a large vehicle, great for family trips and transporting kids to baseball games, but it's ill-suited for driving indoors! I could never bring my van into your home to show it to you. I could, however, bring along the *title,* which is proof that I own it. Our faith is our title, our proof that our relationship with God truly exists. Our faith is the proof, or assurance, of "things hoped for." Our forgiveness and our promise of heaven are real, but we cannot see them. Our faith gives us certainty that we are forgiven and will spend eternity in heaven.

As a kid, I listened to many broadcasts. I knew for certain that the events coming over the airwaves were actually taking place as described in Yankee Stadium. But there in the broadcast booth with Ernie Harwell, I not only heard what was taking place, I could *see* the reality of what was being delivered over the air. Those fans in "radio land" had to accept by faith that Ernie was telling the truth, but I could see for myself that his words were true.

Faith is like that. By faith we try to understand all the things that will become so clear and evident when we gaze into our Lord's face. Faith is the proof—the title deed—of the reality of our future. It is the bridge that takes us from the "here and now" to the "there and then"—from the radio broadcast alone to the reality of the booth during the actual game.

Ed Diaz

EXTRA INNINGS
Read 2 Corinthians 4:16-18

- Describe the differences between what we perceive to be happening and what God says is actually going on in our lives.
- What difficulty in your life will this knowledge help you deal with today?

FIVE

FAIR POLE

THE RIGHT-HANDED HITTER SLAPPED AN OUTSIDE PITCH DOWN THE right field line. Enough of the bat connected to send the ball soaring and slicing toward the foul pole. The crowd rose to its feet and watched as if in slow motion. Inside the foul pole and it's a home run, game over, we win, and we all go home. Outside the pole and it's nothing but a long strike.

Clang! The ball bounced off yellow-painted steel for a homer, and the extra-inning game ended in a home team victory. It all came down to a few inches either way, inside the park or out of bounds. No in between. Fair or foul. Everything hinged on the foul pole.

No Gray Areas Here

Actually, the foul pole is poorly named. It should be called the "fair pole" because it is entirely within the field of play. A ball glancing off the edge of the pole is still a home run.

There are many gray areas in life. We like to argue balls and strikes, safe or out, the greatest hitters of all time. But some areas of life are simply either fair or foul—no in-between, right or wrong, good or bad, truth or error. Consider, for instance, three big questions that we all must answer—and the answers are either fair or foul, with no gray, only black or white: Who

32

is Jesus? What has He done? How will I respond?

Our view of Christ Himself is clearly a black or white issue. Is He the God of the universe or not? In John 8:58-59 a running debate between the Jews and Jesus comes to a head around this crucial matter. Jesus makes a statement, something impossible for a mere mortal to claim.

> *"I tell you the truth," Jesus answered, "before Abraham was born, I am." At this, they picked up stones to stone him, but Jesus hid himself, slipping away. . . .*

The Jewish leaders clearly understood Jesus' claim; He was claiming to be the eternal God. And this clear message angered His enemies to the point of murderous rage. This is one looming fair pole of Christianity. Its height extends into eternity, and every man's theology will fall on one side of it or the other. Is Jesus who He said He was, or not? In John 14:6 Jesus said,

> *"I am the way and the truth and the life. No one comes to the Father except through me."*

The second fair-or-foul question extends beyond who Jesus *is* to what Jesus *does*. Does He really provide eternal salvation? A human being for sure, Jesus is also the true God and offers the only access to the Father. Jesus' unique position—fully God and fully man—allows Him the opportunity to bridge the gap between God and humans. He is *the way*—the only access point to His Father. If we seek a relationship with God, we must come to Him through the only access available—His Son.

Jesus also claims to be *the truth*. There are many dead-end pathways that claim to lead to God. Most of them are sincere, yet all but one are sincerely wrong. Jesus is the true pathway to the Father. Jesus personifies truth.

Jesus' final claim is that He is *the life*. It has been said that we are in the land of the dying going to the land of the living. If we are on Jesus' true pathway we are already experiencing the new life only He can provide. We can have peace with God right now because of Jesus.

The third fair-pole question of life has to do with our destiny. Where will we spend eternity? Romans 6:23 says,

> *For the wages of sin is death but the gift of God is eternal life in Christ Jesus our Lord.*

Our sinful nature has earned us the sentence of death but God has provided His Son Jesus Christ, who is the way, the truth, and the life. Through faith alone in Jesus, God's Son, we can have a new life that starts now and lasts forever.

The fair pole is a deciding line in each ballpark. And our lives have deciding lines, too. We can debate many issues until the early morning hours, but the dividing lines always run through Jesus.

DAN BOLIN

EXTRA INNINGS
READ JOHN 6:35-37

- Why does Jesus describe Himself as food and drink?
- What inner hungers or thirsts do you have that can be satisfied only by Jesus?

SIX

FOUL BALLS

FOUL BALLS WERE THE THRILL OF LITTLE LEAGUE BASEBALL at Trenton Park. It was a grand stadium with a real home run fence, dugouts, a P. A. system, and a concession stand with a snowcone machine.

When a foul ball sailed into the weeds just beyond the right field line, a mad scramble erupted in the stands—youngsters punching, shoving, jumping from the top row, racing madly in pursuit of the ball. The game itself faded into the background for those few moments as boys and girls in the bleachers rushed headlong into weeds and bushes looking for that precious little scuffed-up prize.

What's the Rush?
The motivation was not altruism. The reality was that a foul ball could be exchanged for a free snowcone at the concession stand. Grape, cherry, lime, mixture—you return the ball, you get the cone.

Chasing a baseball with reckless abandon for the prized snowcone gave focus and purpose to the lives of countless kids at Trenton Park over the years. Some of those in the chase wanted the honor of accomplishing where others failed, but most just wanted cool refreshment on a hot day. Do we prize our relationship with Jesus enough to pursue it with such reckless abandon? In Philippians 3:13-14 Paul says,

Forgetting what is behind and straining toward what is ahead, I press on toward the goal to win the prize for which God has called me heavenward in Christ Jesus.

Paul understood the need to forge ahead in his Christian life. But what, exactly, is the goal that drove Paul forward with such focus and desire? And what is Paul's prize?

The goal and the prize are very similar but they each have a different emphasis. A goal focuses attention on the event itself, while a prize rewards a successful result. The goal is to find that foul ball, and the prize is the snowcone.

Chasing the Goal

For Paul, living his entire life for Christ was the great goal. A few verses earlier, he addressed the issue in more detail.

I want to know Christ and the power of his resurrection and the fellowship of sharing in his suffering. (Philippians 3:10)

The goal of Paul's life was to know Christ, to experience God's power, and to share in Christ's suffering. I like parts one and two; to know Christ and to experience His power sound great. But to partner with Christ in suffering isn't too inviting. Yet Paul knew that if the goal was to be like Christ, then Christ's servant would need to identify with the Master's power *and* His pain. Christ experienced His pain at the crucifixion and demonstrated His power in the resurrection. To know Christ requires more than enjoying His fellowship in the good times; it means trusting Him when everything is falling apart.

Winning the Prize

The prize comes after the race has been run. We hold our medals and trophies after the event has concluded and the heat of competition has cooled.

In Paul's time the prize for winning a race was a crown of leaves and flowers. They were beautiful for the moment but they faded quickly. Another race must be run to regain the fading glory of the earlier day. The ultimate prize, the one Paul pursued for so long, would last for eternity. It was the prize of God's comment, "Well done, good and faithful servant" (Matthew 25:23). Paul wanted to stay focused here on earth so he could become as much like Christ as possible, thus gaining a prize that would be of lasting value in heaven.

Chasing foul balls, those little spheres that have so little value, captured the hearts of every wannabe ballplayer hanging around Trenton Park. The goal of every Christian should be the imitation of Christ in His power and in His suffering, because the prize could hardly be more refreshing: hearing the Lord's personal commendation for a job well done.

Dan Bolin

EXTRA INNINGS
READ 2 PETER 3:13-14

- When have you focused more on the past than on the future? Why is it important to keep looking forward?
- What could you do to live "spotless and blameless?"

SEVEN

BRANDENBURG BARBECUE

MY FRIEND GARY BRANDENBURG PLAYED MINOR LEAGUE baseball for three years before giving up his dream of the big leagues and heading off to seminary. Gary tells great stories of life as a minor league catcher in AA Charlotte, North Carolina, but his life wasn't built exclusively around becoming a great ballplayer. Baseball was important to him, but his goals reached even beyond making it to the majors.

Gary also knew how to have fun. Nearing the end of his final season, and not being in the starting lineup, he worked in the bullpen warming up relief pitchers. Instead of complaining about not starting, fuming in the hot sun, or bemoaning the end of his professional career, Gary smuggled a Hibachi barbecue grill down the third base line and into the bullpen (which was just out of the coaches' full view). By the third inning he had grilled enough hot dogs for the whole pitching staff and many of the spectators in the front row.

What's Your Perspective?
Life is full of disappointments—dreams unfulfilled and expectations far from realized. But these painful realities need not shape the landscape of our lives.

Perspective is everything. The apostle Paul saw life from the top and from the bottom.

I have learned to be content whatever the circumstances. I know what it is to be in need, and I know what it is to have plenty. I have learned the secret of being content in any and every situation, whether well fed or hungry, whether living in plenty or in want. I can do everything through him who gives me strength. (Philippians 4:11-13)

Life possessed meaning for Paul when he lived out of his connectedness to Jesus Christ. The high points were great but didn't determine life's essential meaning. The low points created problems for him but didn't control his view of himself, of God, or of the world. The trials and tribulations were merely events within which he could grow in trust and learn to walk more closely with the Lord.

Apparently Paul was like us, because he was required to "learn the secret" of maintaining this perspective. It didn't come naturally to him and, like us, Paul tended to be controlled by his circumstances. When life's events were treating him well he was on top, but when the situation changed he was vulnerable to feelings of discouragement and disappointment. But Paul learned the secret.

Every baseball player wants to make it to the big leagues, but for every one who gets there, thousands are cut along the way. If a player's identity is wrapped up in making it to the next level, and the opportunity passes him by, he'll be severely disappointed, perhaps significantly depressed.

That's why we're called to a better way, to build our

identities upon our relationship with Jesus Christ rather than upon our accomplishments, status, or possessions. Those things can change so quickly. Being united with Christ, however, is the solid foundation upon which we can build an unshakable life of contentment in any situation.

Can You Be Content?
But what does it mean to be "okay" with the way things are— just as they are? Does it call for a kind of mystical, passive acquiescence to life's ups and downs so that we're always thoroughly immune to the events hurtling our way? No, we do live in the real world. We'll feel its depths of joy and sorrow like anyone else. Contentment simply means experiencing a love relationship with God that is stronger—because it is more *essential,* more foundational—than any problem the world can send us. We are not required to perform to a prescribed level, accomplish a great feat, or obtain a challenging goal to know that we are loved by God. We can be content in that relationship and use it as a launching pad to do the tasks that He sets before us— all while learning the easy or difficult lessons that every circumstance can teach us.

The ability to ride out the highs and lows of life is tied to our relationship with God, a blessed reality that transcends the bumps and blessings of daily living. Nevertheless, most of us are controlled more by our ability to find a close-in parking spot on a hot day than by the reality of our union with Christ. Perhaps that is why Paul sees this key principle of life as a secret.

The secret is not difficult to understand, but it is very

difficult to apply. Most of the time we're overwhelmed by wins and losses, mostly not very focused on our relationship with God. Yet the next time a dream fizzles or a disappointment comes our way we might remember that, no matter what our response, we can do nothing to make God love us more and we can do nothing to make God love us less.

Then we realize that circumstances could be better—but they could be worse. Then we can break out the Hibachi and barbecue some hot dogs. After all, a few other of life's "players" may need some encouragement, as well.

DAN BOLIN

EXTRA INNINGS
READ HEBREWS 13:5-6

- What does our love of money tell us about our contentment with our relationship to God?
- How does "God is our helper" give you confidence to face the tasks before you today?

EIGHT

GIVE ME THE BALL!

MY OLDEST SON IS A LEFT-HANDED PITCHER. HE'S HAD GREAT success both in high school and in college, but his greatest attribute is his desire to pitch at "crunch time." Many pitchers are willing to throw when things are going well, but it is the unique individual who wants the ball when the big game is on the line.

Zach is that kind of player.

Always Ready?
I became keenly aware of this during Zach's senior year of high school. We had battled for three years to win a state championship. We had progressed from losing in the semi-finals the first year to losing in the finals the next. Once again we were ready to play for the state championship—against the number-five ranked team in the nation.

Coach Carpenter and I faced a difficult decision: when to throw Zach. Would it be better to use him in the semi-finals and be reasonably certain we'd have a chance to reach the title game? Or would it be best to save Zach for the championship game?

As we discussed all the possible pitching combinations, Zach was in the batting cage. He overheard us talking and

calmly approached. "I have one thing I'd like to say," he inter-
rupted. "If we're playing in the championship game, I don't
want to be stuck playing first base unable to pitch!"

Coming from my soft-spoken son, this quiet statement was
the equivalent of a bombshell. Simply put, Zach wanted the
ball in the title game. That made our decision easy. We would
save Zach as best we could for the final game.

Things didn't work exactly as we hoped they would. Zach
had to throw three innings the night before in the semi-finals
to salvage our chances to play for the championship, but he
still wanted the ball in the final game. He showed great forti-
tude and held our rivals to three hits over seven innings. He got
the win, and we took home our first state title. Zach had been
ready, willing, and able.

No Guarantee

However, being ready, willing, and able doesn't always guarantee success. One year later, Zach was the freshman bullpen
stopper in the College World Series for Florida State University.
Zach had led the Seminoles in appearances and was especially
effective with men on base. Eight times during his freshman
season, Zach had been called upon to enter a ball game with
the bases loaded. Eight times Zach was able to find the strike
zone and escape without a run being scored. Eight times Zach
had wanted the ball and was successful—until now.

When Coach Mike Martin motioned to the bullpen for
Zach to face the best hitter on a rival team during the opening
game in Omaha, twenty-two thousand people waited, along
with Zach's parents. Zach was exactly *where* he wanted to be,

doing *what* he did best. He had prepared in every way for this moment. Yet on a 1-1 pitch Zach threw a change-up, which the batter quickly deposited in the right field seats. We were devastated. Zach was disappointed. His team lost the game. But he wanted the ball again the very next day.

No doubt Zach had begun to understand the principle of Proverbs 21:31, which says,

The horse is prepared for the day of battle, but victory belongs to the Lord.

Zach had done a terrific job of preparing himself to pitch. But preparation is no guarantee of victory. Victory on the battle field (or playing field) ultimately belongs to the Lord.

Nevertheless, Be Prepared

Perhaps you're facing a battle in your own life right now. Perhaps you're struggling in your marriage or with your finances or on your job. Solomon would want to know how you have prepared for the day of battle: Have you done all that God would want you to do in this situation? Have you ultimately laid the situation and its results in His mighty hands? If you have done your very best in God's eyes, then that is all you can do. In fact, that is all God expects from you. It is our job to prepare diligently, then to trust God with the results.

Zach recovered wonderfully. Although his freshman season ended in disappointment, he went on to be named an All-American that summer in the NBC World Series. The next season he was named to the All-ACC team. He hopes to become the all-time leader in appearances for Florida State during his senior season.

Simply put, Zach is prepared. He works out daily to increase his strength, speed, and skill. He has not stopped doing his very best. He still wants the ball. Do you?

ED DIAZ

EXTRA INNINGS
READ 1 TIMOTHY 6:11-16

- What is it about God's nature that should motivate us to diligently work for Him and trust Him with the results?
- What battle are you presently facing? Have you prepared diligently? Are you entrusting the results to God? How do you know?

NINE

WATCH THE WATCH

MY SECOND SON, MATTE, IS A GREAT BASEBALL PLAYER.
More specifically, he's a great hitter. He recently set the record
for home runs hit by a freshman at Florida State University.
What an incredible joy it was to watch MattE hit four home
runs in one ball game to tie an NCAA record!

It's easy for fans watching him to overlook the hard work
that has gone into MattE's hitting ability. To be sure, God has
blessed him with wonderful hand/eye coordination and terrific
eyesight. However, other areas of the game have been a struggle
for him, especially in his youth.

Left or Right?
We were surprised and a bit disappointed to find that MattE
had dyslexia. This became evident as he was learning to print
in kindergarten. His numbers and letters were often backward
and easily transposed. MattE dealt well with his problem, and
my wife worked diligently with him until he was able to read
and perform well academically. But as he grew, the problem of
knowing right from left stayed with him.

We used to draw an arrow on his right gym shoe when he

was young, so he'd be able to distinguish his right foot from his left. That way, in the midst of a heated soccer match, if the coach yelled, "Go right!" MattE could look down at his shoes and quickly proceed in the direction of the arrow. He knew that "Go left!" meant to head in the direction of the unmarked shoe. Most of the world didn't know that MattE had real difficulty in this area. In fact, as he entered high school, his dyslexia provided an interesting exchange between MattE and his new baseball coach.

Early in the season the coach instituted "signs" that each player had to know before he could step into the batter's box. Coach Carpenter went over each sign thoroughly. The signs were tricky, because a movement with the left hand could mean something totally different from the same movement with the right hand. Coach then tested the players in the dugout to ensure they had a handle on each sign.

One by one, each player seemed to grasp the new signals from their coach. When he concluded, Coach Carpenter asked if there were any questions. MattE slowly raised his hand. "Coach, during the games, are you always going to be wearing your watch on your left hand?" he wanted to know.

The coach responded with surprise, "Probably. I hadn't really thought about it. Why do you ask?"

Sheepishly, MattE said, "Because then I can tell which hand is your right hand and which is your left."

Well, as you might guess, the dugout erupted with laughter. After things calmed down, the coach responded gently, "Sure, I'll wear the watch, MattE. In fact, if you will just 'watch the watch' you'll always know which hand is my left hand."

Paying Attention?

It was important for MattE to watch the watch in order to understand the signals that Coach Carpenter was giving during the intensity of a baseball game. It is even more important that we, as Christians, pay attention to the signals, which our heavenly Father gives us in our walk with Him. In 1 Thessalonians 5, the apostle Paul begins a series of commands (signals, if you will, from the coaching box):

> *Verse 16—Rejoice always.*
> *Verse 17—Pray without ceasing.*
> *Verse 18—In everything give thanks.*
> *Verse 19—Do not quench the Spirit.*

I can just imagine our heavenly Father standing in the third base box flashing these signs to us in the midst of the intensity of our lives, hoping we will glance over and follow His instructions.

Though each command is important, the one that jumps out at me comes in verse 17:

> *Pray without ceasing.*

Just what does that mean and just how often do we obey it?

Still Hacking Away?

The phrase "without ceasing" comes from a Greek root word that refers to a child with a hacking cough. If you have ever been up at night with a sick child, you know just how unrelenting that kind of cough can be. Just about the time you begin nodding off to sleep, there comes that cough again. God commands us to pray in the same constant way. We are to pray without ceasing—as though we have a hacking cough that won't quit.

Next time you feel yourself stepping into the batter's box in your spiritual life, look over at the third base coaching box. What is God telling you to do? You are never left to guess on your own. God is the ultimate coach. He knows what to do in every situation, and He's always there giving you a "sign." One thing you can be sure of: He's telling you to keep praying.

MattE grew up to be a terrific baseball player. In the last game of his high school career, he was able to steal third base at a critical time. Understanding the coach's signal, and obeying it, led to a win for his team. Knowing the signs and being willing to put them into practice—"without ceasing"—is essential to victory in our walk with God.

ED DIAZ

EXTRA INNINGS
READ PSALM 25:4-5

- What would you like God to reveal to you today?
- Write down a verse that has been significant in your life. What guidance does God want to provide in your life today through that verse?

MOST VALUABLE "PICKER"

ONE OF THE MOST IMPORTANT PLAYERS ON OUR HIGH SCHOOL club seldom entered a single game. As a matter of fact, he was once awarded our "MVP of the Game" title without ever leaving the bench.

Tex, you see, had a unique ability to decipher the opponent's signs. Usually by the beginning of the second inning he was able to "pick" their signs, alerting our hitters to what pitch was coming. He was often able to inform us before an opposing runner attempted to steal a base. Tex was willing to turn his long hours on the bench into a real asset. He was a true servant, ready to sacrifice his time for the good of the team.

Servanthood and Sacrifice

Baseball is a game of servanthood and sacrifice, though it is certainly unique in its use of the word "sacrifice." You just don't find this terminology in football. Have you ever heard of a "sacrifice block"? Or a "sacrifice free throw" in basketball? But each day our high school players practice sacrifice bunts. Sometimes the deciding run in a big game can score on a sacrifice fly.

So baseball has many servants. Behind-the-scenes servanthood and sacrifice are as important at the ballpark as the plays on the field. Dozens of people, from groundskeepers to scoreboard operators to bus drivers, serve virtually unnoticed.

Many things go into creating a successful ball club, but the willingness to serve and sacrifice is one of the most important intangibles. Whether it's by a home run hitter called to lay down a bunt to move a teammate from first to second or a clubhouse helper who is asked to tape a bat, servanthood and sacrifice are vital to the game.

Incentive and Ability

In John 13, Jesus, who was about to become our ultimate sacrifice, teaches His disciples an important lesson about servanthood by washing their feet. But before He washes one foot, John 13:3 says,

> *Jesus, knowing that the Father had given all things into His hands, and that He had come forth from God, and was going back to God . . .*

In this verse, we become aware that Christ knew some things that gave Him the incentive and ability to serve. First, He knew "that the Father had given all things into His hands." That is, He knew how much He was worth to God. It didn't matter what others thought of Him; God was willing to give Him *everything*. Understanding His true value gave Him a *dignity* that allowed Him to serve others.

Second, He knew that He had been sent forth from God. Jesus knew where He was from—not merely from Bethlehem or Nazareth or Galilee. He knew that He was the Father's representative. Understanding His true *identity*, He was free to wash the feet of His disciples.

Finally, Jesus was "going back to God." He knew where He was headed. This gave Him tremendous *security.* Because Christ knew that His ultimate destination was not the cross or the tomb—but the throne room of God, He was free to serve.

How about you? Do you understand that as a believer in Christ you have a new self-worth? Your self-esteem is not tied to a batting average or salary figure. It is tied to your position in Christ.

In one of our biggest high school games, the opposing team was doing a masterful job of hiding their signs. Through the first several innings we were being shut out, and a loss would have eliminated us from the play-offs. In about the fifth inning, however, Tex broke the code! From that point on we began to pound the opposing pitcher and were able to score enough runs to advance to the state finals. To be sure, the players on the field deserved credit for executing their duties. But our MVP that day was Tex—Most Valuable "Picker." Because of his diligent willingness to serve his team, Tex helped us advance into the championship game.

Who on your "team" needs your sacrificial help today?

ED DIAZ

EXTRA INNINGS
READ EPHESIANS 6:7-8

- When we serve others, who are we really serving?
- How are we to serve others on our "team"?

ELEVEN

SECOND CHANCES

BASEBALL IS A GAME ABOUT GRACE. A BATTER SWINGS AND misses . . . and he gets another chance. With two strikes he may foul off as many pitches as he wants with no penalty. If he makes an out, he can bat again in a couple of innings. If the team loses, they have a chance to play again tomorrow. When the season ends without a championship, the cliché is true: "There's always next year."

That's what's great about spring training: the losses of last season are wiped clean; the earned runs given up by pitchers the year before aren't considered in the new season; fielding errors are a thing of the past; and strikeouts from former seasons aren't held against any hitters. Make no mistake, bad habits and poor play are still a part of each player's total performance, and each player must strive to improve, but the record of past wrongs is done away with and the slate is wiped clean.

Yes, second chances are handed out liberally in baseball. It's surely one of the attractions drawing so many of us to identify with the game. We know we need second chances in life, as well.

Before We Were Worthy . . .
That's what grace is: second chances. Not because we are worthy, but quite the opposite. God chooses to demonstrate

53

His grace to us when we are the most undeserving so that He can show His wonderful and merciful character to us.

Because of our unworthiness grace is grace. Romans 5 gives us a clear picture of the grace that God has demonstrated to us.

> *You see, at just the right time, when we were still power-less, Christ died for the ungodly.* (Verse 6)

God's grace was ultimately displayed in the death of His Son, Jesus. The penalty for our sins was completely paid when Jesus, the perfect sacrifice, took our punishment in our place. He substituted Himself for us so that we could escape the judgment that we would otherwise face without hope.

Why would anyone die in the place of another and put himself through such pain? The beneficial results are awesome, but the price seems very high. Verse 7 gives us a clue:

> *Very rarely will anyone die for a righteous man, though for a good man someone might possibly dare to die.*

Sometimes a person is willing to exchange his life for a good man, but this is very rare. As in any event, the value of the other human being isn't the driving force that moves a person to such an heroic act. The only real motivation is the giver's own deep love for the one in need. Demonstrating the massive reservoir of love for us is what moved Jesus to act as He did to give us a second chance.

> *God demonstrated his own love for us in this: While we were sinners, Christ died for us.*

Baseball just happened to develop around the idea of second

chances, but God was very intentional with His plan. He wanted to show His love in a way that would overwhelm us with the depth of His passionate care and concern. So instead of waiting until we had cleaned up our act, He took the initiative and showed His love before we were worthy.

He Took the Initiative

What can we do with such great news but respond with overflowing love and devotion?

> *We . . . rejoice in God through our Lord Jesus Christ, through whom we have now received reconciliation.* (Romans 5:11)

Reconciliation means to stop fighting and establish a friendship. That's what God's grace and second chances are all about. He took the initiative to open the door for a relationship. Our challenge is to accept His free and loving gift and enjoy a friendship with Him. We do that by simply trusting Him and accepting our undeserved acceptance.

DAN BOLIN

EXTRA INNINGS
READ ROMANS 8:1-4

- How do you interpret the phrase "he condemned sin in sinful man"? What does "no condemnation" mean to you?
- What is the most wonderful second chance you've received from God so far? How have you shown your gratitude?

TWELVE

HOME FIELD ADVANTAGE

EVERY BALLPARK HAS ITS DISTINCTIVE DESIGN AND SPECIAL configuration, making each baseball game unique. Whether the wind is blowing in or out will determine whether a player is a home run hitter or just another guy with warning-track power. Infield grass allowed to grow tall will slow ground balls and provide an aging shortstop a reasonable chance to make a play.

The various shapes and sizes of ballparks also give each game its own personality. Symmetry, or lack thereof, can create unusual situations. For example, the right and left field corners can be a real challenge. The location of bullpens and rolled-up rain tarps can also make for interesting moments. Because of these variations, the home team always has an advantage when an opposing outfielder chases a ball into a corner and is suddenly caught off guard by a crazy carom.

Baseball has remained virtually the same game for a hundred years. Yet each game is different and exciting in its own way, due, at least in part, to the ballpark itself.

Establishing the Home Field
Knowing the details of the ballpark adds up to a big advantage, but also having the crowd on their side provides players

with a surge of adrenaline. Clearly, playing on a home field has mental and emotional advantages.

Have you ever considered that, as fathers, we are charged with establishing a "home field advantage" for our children? This involves providing opportunities for our children to develop spiritually and a place for them to receive encouragement and support. One of the greatest passages dealing with a father's role of establishing this kind of home field advantage is found in Deuteronomy 6:6-8.

> *These commandments that I give you today are to be upon your hearts. Impress them on your children. Talk about them when you sit at home and when you walk along the road, when you lie down and when you get up.*

The passage starts with the heart of the father. What is on your heart? Is it the commandments of God? If we are to give our children an advantage and set them on a pathway toward God, we must first walk that pathway ourselves. The example we set overpowers the words we say. Children need to *see* us following God as we speak to them about heading in the same direction.

Children are very impressionable, and the Scripture says we should use that to our best advantage. We need to impress them with the things of God at every opportunity, and we can impress them most effectively up close. In other words, we need to be involved in their lives, constantly watching for moments when they're ready to be instructed in the things of God. The passage says that any place is the right place and any time is the right time for a "teachable moment." At home or on the road together, we can teach our children. When we go to sleep or when we get up we can instruct those who will lead the next generation.

Supplying the "Crowd"

But teaching our children the instructions of God's Word is only one part of the job of establishing a home field advantage for them. Conveying knowledge about the playing field and its special features is one part of the challenge; the other part is providing the encouragement of a hometown crowd. Ephesians 6:4 says,

Fathers, do not exasperate your children.

Nothing disappoints and leaves a child more unfulfilled and frustrated than to be neglected by his or her father. Dads need to be interested in the details of their children's lives. They need to be at ball games, recitals, and school functions. They need to be their children's biggest fan, cheering them on, day by day.

A warm, loving relationship opens the door for conversations that will lead into spiritual matters. Yes, it takes a determined commitment to sacrifice time and other opportunities to invest in the lives of our children, but in doing so we impress them for life.

What an advantage for such children!

Life will take some crazy bounces, and things won't always turn out the way we anticipate. But we must help our sons and daughters prepare for a life of loving, obeying, and serving God with all the advantage we can provide. It starts with molding our own hearts. It requires huge amounts of time. And it involves establishing a secure environment for conversations to unfold—blessed off-the-cuff dialogs that will make a difference for the life and eternity of a child.

DAN BOLIN

EXTRA INNINGS
READ PSALM 78:1-7

- How would you describe the "home field advantage" in your family of origin? How strong is it in your own family these days?
- How many generations are described in these verses? What are the desired results in verse 7? How do you apply this passage to your own life?

LOUISVILLE SLUGGER

IN THE DAYS BEFORE THE "PING" OF METAL BATS RESOUNDED across our nation's ball fields, the music of amateur baseball included the crack of a fastball exploding off a wooden Louisville Slugger.

Each Louisville Slugger bat comes inscribed with the name of a professional, super-star hitter branded into the meaty part of the bat's barrel. To become a great hitter it seems you need a bat bearing the name of an all-star at least—and better yet, a Hall of Fame slugger. The name is little more than a marketing ploy, but to a Babe Ruth wannabe the signature identifies even the weakest swinging novice with the greatest of the heavy-hitting heroes.

Implementing Imitating

Just as young players desire to imitate their favorite baseball heroes, we are to imitate God Himself. But what does this look like? How do we go about trying to imitate Christ? Ephesians 5 gives us five clues. The first way we imitate God is through love. Verse 2 tells us,

> *Live a life of love, just as Christ loved us and gave himself up for us.*

God's love for us is at the center of His character. If we are to imitate Christ we must demonstrate love to those around us. And like Christ we must show love to those who are unlovely.

The next clue, in verse 3, is sexual purity:

But among you there must not even be the hint of sexual immorality.

God is pure in every sense of the word. He expects those who imitate Him also to be pure in all areas of life, but especially in the area of sexual relations. We will destroy our opportunity to serve God in every other way if we fail to imitate God's pattern of purity. The third clue to implementing a life of godly imitation comes in verse 8:

Live as children of light (for the fruit of the light consists in all goodness, righteousness and truth).

We are to look for ways to produce godly fruit in our lives. Living as children of light means finding opportunities to do good, righteous, and truthful acts. These may arise in any area of life: at home, at work, at church. Wherever the opportunity, we can attempt to produce a godly act of service.

The fourth clue comes in verse 15:

Be very careful, then, how you live—not as unwise but as wise, making the most of every opportunity, because the days are evil.

There is too much evil in the world to miss chances to say and do things for God. God leaves us on earth to do His will and to develop a godly character. Wise living is proactive in finding ways to invest ourselves so we can impact the world and grow at the same time.

The final issue is submission, found in verse 21:

Submit to one another out of reverence for Christ.

To imitate Christ means taking a lowly position. Jesus didn't try to exalt Himself but was willing to lower Himself to the point of dying so that we could live with Him. This may be the toughest challenge of the five. We want to be in charge, controlling others rather than submitting to them. But humbly submitting ourselves to one another is crucial if we truly desire to imitate God.

Love, purity, godly acts of service, wisdom, and submission are not the only activities that God expects of us as we imitate Him. But doing these things gives us a good start on the road to spiritual maturity.

Like the children who strive to imitate their sports heroes, we should make every effort to become as much like God as possible. What could be better than having God's image stamped upon the day-to-day activities of our lives?

DAN BOLIN

EXTRA INNINGS
READ MATTHEW 22:16-22

- What or whose image is stamped on your heart of hearts?
- If our life is stamped with the image of God Himself, what are we to do?

TAKE THE FIRST PITCH

I WAS IN MY EARLY FORTIES WHEN I TOOK MY DAUGHTER TO the batting cage. She was a fine young third base girl on a co-ed Little League team. She hit well in two years of T-ball and one year of coach pitch, but when real opponents started throwing heat she needed some extra help.

She hit well at forty-five miles per hour. I kept stuffing quarters into the money box, and for fifty cents another ten pitches would come firing toward home plate.

"Swing hard."

"Keep your head in."

"Don't drop your shoulder."

"Good cut."

I used all of the usual dadisms to help her improve and to encourage her on.

She tired of swinging before my pocket of quarters ran out, so I put on a helmet, grabbed a bat, and stepped into the cage to show her how it was done.

This time she set the machine on sixty-five miles per hour, dropped in the quarters, and I was ready. Slowly the arm rotated into position, picked up a baseball, and let it fly in my direction.

That's when it happened.

Incredibly, I stood there and watched the first pitch go by. Why would I waste money not swinging at the first pitch from a batting machine? The answer slammed into my consciousness. Dad always told me, "Take the first pitch; size up the pitcher, gauge the speed of the ball, and make the guy prove he can throw a strike."

I had this flashback, a memory moment of amazement. What my dad told me more than thirty years earlier had controlled my actions as an adult without my realizing it. About then the second pitch flew past the plate.

"Are you okay, Dad?"

"Yeah, sure." Then I swung late on pitch number three. Fouling off two was as close as I got to a hit. But I had taken the first pitch.

How Do You Speak to Them?

Fathers' words are incredibly powerful. As dads, we must recognize that we are setting expectations, influencing perspectives, and instilling patterns that will be carried with our sons and daughters throughout their lives. Children have free wills and the ability to choose, but how they view themselves, the world, and God Himself will be shaped to a great degree by a father's comments.

In Matthew 3:17 we find the account of Jesus' baptism in the River Jordan. In the midst of this event God the Father speaks from heaven,

This is my Son, whom I love; with him I am well pleased.

Can you think of a greater compliment for a father to give

his child? This sentence speaks of three crucial issues any dad should consider when addressing his children. First is the issue of *identity*. God the Father is quick to say, "That's my boy!" Dads breathe strength and confidence into a child when they go out of their way to identify with a son or daughter. Somehow the attributes of Dad are shared with the developing child in a powerful way when dads and children connect. Attending ball games, watching school plays, fishing together, as well as offering timely words of affirmation will help you identify you with your child.

Second is the issue of *whom I love*. When our children know that we love them more than life itself, they settle down into contentment and security. Our children need to know—and *feel*—that we love them just because they are our children, not because of good grades, proper behavior, or the home runs they hit in ball games. The more we communicate our love to our children, the more they are freed from performance-based attempts to earn our love. Love is not a noun to be earned but a verb to be experienced. Children need to know that we love them through the good times and the tough times of life, especially when they make bad decisions and silly mistakes. Even when we are disciplining them, they should have no doubt they're loved.

Finally, when God the Father said, *with him I am well pleased,* He affirmed the quality of His Son's activities. We, too, will encourage our children's good choices and proper use of the gifts entrusted to them. This affirmation of their performance is not the same as expressing our unfailing love for them. Rather it is a statement of support—they are using the platform we have provided to approach and impact the world.

God the Father made a powerful statement about His Son; He identified with Him, loved Him, and supported Him. We're given the same awesome privilege. We can follow the Father's example and direct strong statements toward our children to influence them for a lifetime.

DAN BOLIN

EXTRA INNINGS
READ PROVERBS 16:21-24

- What are the positive and negative implications of the words we speak?
- What impact will your words have on those closest to you today?

FIFTEEN

A PHENOMENAL PHAILURE

NICKNAMES ARE A VITAL PART OF BASEBALL LORE. IN EVERY decade a few stand out. "Joltin' Joe" and "The Splendid Splinter" were two of the best to play the game. Entire teams had nicknames—"The Gas House Gang" and "The Bronx Bombers" played in St. Louis and New York respectively. There were "Yogi" Berra and Stan "The Man" Musial; Leo "The Lip" Durocher, and Harry "The Hat" Walker. The two greatest home run hitters of all time were nicknamed "Hammerin' Hank" Aaron and "Babe" Ruth. From "Yaz" to "Maz," the game has been full of descriptive monikers.

But you've probably never heard of "Phenomenal" Smith. As a twenty-year-old, he played for the Brooklyn Bridegrooms in the old American Association way back in 1885. The fact that John Francis Gammon Smith endowed himself with the title "Phenomenal" tells you a lot about his personality. Apparently, he chose this nickname after pitching a no-hitter for Newark in the Eastern League. When he was brought up to the big leagues, Phenomenal boasted to his new teammates about his prowess. He informed them that he was a great pitcher—so great that he wouldn't even need their help to win. (Apparently his IQ wasn't much higher than his ERA.)

Needing No Help?

In fact, he didn't get their help at all. Although he pitched well in his major league debut against the St. Louis Cardinals, giving up no earned runs, he suffered an 18-5 shellacking. The Brooklyn ball club committed fourteen errors behind their arrogant new pitcher—most of them intentional! And that doesn't take into account the number of balls that were allowed to roll past the infield or drop untouched into the outfield.

The next day, the *Brooklyn Eagle* newspaper condemned the entire ball club. In fact, each of the players who participated in the fiasco was fined five hundred dollars by team management (a hefty sum in those days). Charles Byrne, the president of the baseball team, was forced to release Phenomenal Smith in order to ensure domestic tranquillity. This twenty-year-old phenomenon turned out to be a phenomenal phailure.

No one questioned Phenomenal Smith's talent and ability on the playing field. However, his failure came as a result of his boasting in the clubhouse. Boasting is a dangerous disease when it comes to the game of baseball. As coaches, we tell our high school players, "Don't get too excited when you win, and don't get too down on yourself when you lose."

The game of baseball is very much like the game of life. It's meant to be played over the long haul. It's a marathon, not a sprint. It's a sport that demands endurance. In what other game can a player fail seven out of ten times and be considered a great success? Even the greatest hitters struggle to hit over .300. Even the greatest teams lose sixty or more times in one season. Boasting can only get a player in trouble. We encourage our high school players to let their play on the field do their talking for them, because sooner or later over the long haul, the game will jump up and restore their humility.

Boasting Just Doesn't Help!

Scripture mentions boasting in a number of places. Ephesians 2:8-9 says we are

> *saved by grace through faith and that not of [ourselves], it is the gift of God; not as a result of works, that no one should boast.*

Even our faith is a gift from our heavenly Father, lest we be tempted to boast that we have earned our way to heaven. Heaven is God's gift to us—a gift we receive by His grace through our faith, which He bestows on us.

It's natural to want to boast about our accomplishments— a spectacular play we once made or a winning team we played on. (Phenomenal Smith continued to brag about his ability. In fact, he won only fifty-seven games and lost seventy-eight during his ensuing major league career.) However, the Bible only mentions one good cause for boasting. Jeremiah 9:23-24 tells us not to boast in our own abilities but only in the fact that we have a relationship with God.

> *Thus says the LORD, "Let not a wise man boast of his wisdom and let not the mighty man boast of his might, let not a rich man boast of his riches; but let him who boasts boast of this, that he understands and knows Me, that I am the LORD who exercises lovingkindness, justice, and*

righteousness on earth; for I delight in these things," declares the LORD.

Paul, in 1 Corinthians 1:31, reiterates this message:

Let him who boasts, boast in the Lord.

In other words, it's okay to brag about the goodness and grace of our Savior because it will be a form of worship that we offer with thankful hearts. Any other boasting can lead to phenomenal phailure.

Phenomenal Smith had great success as a AA player in Newark, but that was before he threw his first pitch in the big leagues for Brooklyn. Because of his boasting, he didn't stand a chance. Because of his boasting, you'd probably never even heard of him—until now!

ED DIAZ

EXTRA INNINGS
READ PSALM 12:1-6

- List at least three ways unfaithful people use their tongues.
- Re-read verse 6. How should our tongues be used?

SIXTEEN

PAINTBALLS AND PRIORITIES

IT WAS THE LAST WEEKEND OF THE 1995 MAJOR LEAGUE baseball season. The Detroit Tigers had endured a long season and were well on their way to a hundred losses. The schedule makers had them playing out their final three-game string in Baltimore, facing an Orioles team with great potential but which had also not played up to its pre-season expectations.

Since I'd been invited to do chapel for both ball clubs on the final Sunday of the regular season, I decided to fly in to Baltimore for the series. I arrived at Camden Yard on Thursday afternoon. But to my surprise, none of the Detroit Tigers were in their hotel rooms as they normally would have been.

After several hours, most of the members of the ball club straggled in through the lobby—looking worse than I had ever seen them. *Wow. This season has really been rough on these guys,* I thought to myself. *They look terrible.* Yet I knew that Thursday had been a rare "off day" in the schedule. The players should have been more rested and relaxed than normal.

Best Use of the Time?
Quietly the news leaked out. One of the players had organized an all-day excursion to the Maryland countryside for a time of male bonding—translate that into "paintball wars." A day-long

battle had ensued between the pitchers and the position players. Most of those involved had never participated in infantry combat. As a result, few were prepared for the test of endurance they experienced that day. Most players escaped with minor bruises, but a few had serious scrapes and scratches from the thorns and thistles in the underbrush. The pitchers' legs were particularly sore from the running, racing up and down hills all day. A group of battered but bonded warriors limped into the lobby that evening—and I was the only one in on their secret.

The Orioles swept the Tigers in three straight games. Not only did the Tiger bats go silent, but their pitching was atrocious. One by one the Detroit hurlers trudged in from the bullpen on wobbly legs, and one by one they got rocked. Meanwhile, Baltimore wags extolled the virtues of the Orioles' staff for their ability to hold in check the vaunted Detroit offense. No one except me knew that the Tiger hitters came to the plate with torn, tender hands and bruised, aching shoulders. Many of the Oriole pitchers were offered contract extensions, some with bonuses, based in part on their ability to defeat the Detroit Tigers during that last weekend.

Little did anyone know that the Baltimore victories had been secured by a paintball war earlier in the week! The Detroit management would have been very upset if they had gotten wind of what took place on Thursday prior to the final series. Granted, it was the players' day off, and I'm sure none of their contracts included "paintball wars" on the list of prohibited activities. So technically the way they chose to use their free time that day was not wrong. However, it was certainly unwise. They'd been given the day off to rest and recuperate, in order to be at their best for the final series of the regular season. Instead, they had worn themselves out, making a farce of their final games.

A Better Use of the Time

Paul, in Ephesians 5:15-17, warns Christians about the frivolous use of their time.

Therefore be careful how you walk, not as unwise men, but as wise, making the most of your time, because the days are evil. So then do not be foolish, but understand what the will of the Lord is.

Some translations actually say that we are to "redeem" the time that God has given us. God gives each of us the same amount of time each day, just as an employer credits each of his workers the same amount of pay at the end of a shift. But each of us can choose to dispense of it differently. Some of us spend our time wisely, consuming it on worthy accomplishments with lasting value. Some of us squander it on trivial pursuits. Probably none of those activities would be considered wrong (out of line with our "contract" as Christians), but most of them would be viewed as "unwise" by God.

Both the Tigers and the Orioles had been given a day off. The Orioles used their time wisely—resting and getting ready for their final series. They knew that this was their priority and the wisest use of their time.

Take a moment right now to look back over your calendar. How much of your time this past week has been used wisely, the way God would want you to use it? Would He extend your contract—with a bonus—based on how you've spent your time for Him?

Ed Diaz

- Paul summarizes his life in terms of a boxing match ("I have fought the good fight") and a marathon race ("I have finished the race"). How do you hope to be able to summarize your life? (You may want to use baseball terminology.)
- If Jesus were to physically accompany you through your tasks today, which ones would He spend more time on? Which ones would He spend less time on? How would He evaluate the day you have planned?

SEVENTEEN

SPRING TRAINING

HAVE YOU EVER WONDERED WHY BASEBALL IS SO SPECIAL—how it has become known as America's pastime? In my opinion, it's because the game has so many unique aspects. For instance, it's one of the few games played without a time clock. Each team receives the same number of outs, no matter how long the competition takes. The rules of substitution are unique to baseball as well. While most other sports have "free substitution," in baseball, once a player is substituted for, he cannot re-enter the game. Also, baseball is probably the only major professional sport that feeds not only its players, but the *media* covering each game. What fun to be invited to the clubhouse "spread" before, during, or after a ball game!

But I think the most unique thing about baseball is the very idea of spring training. Other sports teams play "exhibition games," to be sure. But no other sport brings an entourage of support staff, fans, and players clear across the country each winter for two full months—just to get ready for the real games that begin in April.

Spring training season is my favorite part of the year. It's the one special time when fans can get close to the players both on and off the field. The crack of wooden bats and the smell of freshly mowed grass seem to linger in the air longer in the spring than at any other time. It is the exciting, dream-filled time when all the teams are still undefeated and everyone is about to contend for the pennant.

A Practice Run—In Life?

Yes, spring training is a tremendous part of baseball. But I've been thinking: Wouldn't it be grand if life had spring training—a chance to spend the first twenty years getting ready for our real lives, the years that would really count?

This spring training era of life would take place after the playground days of our youth, just as real spring training follows the growing years of Little League and college ball. That way we would be able to practice real life issues as adults, just as the major leaguers do. However, none of the consequences of our decision-making would count toward our "real life" stats.

I would have done some things differently in my life if I'd experienced a spring training. I probably wouldn't have moved as many times, for instance. And some of the mistakes I made with my children would be guilt-free, since I'd have a chance to do them all over again for keeps. I'd also learn to be a better husband, practicing during my spring training so that later on I would be more loving and perhaps more conscious of my wife's needs. I might even consider making different career choices that would better equip me for the present job God has called me to.

But it just doesn't work that way.

There is no spring training for real life. In fact, Hebrews 9:27 says:

It is appointed for men to die once, and after this comes judgment.

Although the verse states that all of us will die once, it also implies that we only get one chance to live. Reincarnation is not an option. There is no spring training. This is our one and only shot. Everything counts.

One Chance to Do It Right

In Psalm 90, Moses looks back at the years he had lived and concludes in verse 10, "as for the days of our life, they contain seventy years, or if due to strength, eighty years." But the real lesson he has for us is found in verse 12:

So teach us to number our days, that we may present to Thee a heart of wisdom.

A "heart of wisdom" is a wonderful concept coming to us from the Old Testament. The word *wisdom* can be literally translated "to live life with skill." The word is used in Exodus 28:3 to describe the man who made garments for the priests. This man went into the fields to cut the flax. Having harvested it, he spun it into thread, wove the thread into cloth, then cut, dyed, and sewed the cloth to make a wonderful garment. Just as the artistic tailor produced an ornate, priestly robe, a wise person is able to make something beautiful out of his life. But as Moses reminds us, we only have one opportunity to do this.

The apostle Paul in the New Testament picks up this same idea. In Colossians 1:23 he reminds us,

Whatever you do, do your work heartily as for the Lord rather than for men; knowing that from the Lord you will receive the reward of the inheritance. It is the Lord Christ whom you serve.

Yes, our days are filled with chances for "do overs" and we experience many gracious redemptions from our mistakes and failings over the years. But all of our experiences need to keep leading us upward toward a closer fellowship with the Lord. Because, as both Moses and Paul understood, when life is considered as a "complete game," we only get to play one of them. We have one opportunity to walk with God on the earth—and this is it!

The big question is this: *How are you spending your days?*

ED DIAZ

EXTRA INNINGS
READ JAMES 3:13-16

- What characteristics accompany a life lived "wisely"?
- Which one of these characteristics will you ask God to display in your life today?

EIGHTEEN

POKE IN THE EYE

I WAS TOO YOUNG TO JOIN THE LITTLE LEAGUE TEAM WITH my older brother, but I had been around baseball all of my life (about seven years) and really wanted to play. That's when I saw the poster in Columbia Park announcing a special softball league for kids my age, so I signed up.

The first practice was just that—practice. We were in two lines tossing the oversized balls back and forth, fielding ground balls and catching pop flies. I was ready to play, but we didn't even get batting practice. The next practice was more of the same, but we also got to hit and run the bases. More action but not the game-playing experience I had expected.

The third time we got together we began with the same routine, but then one of the coaches yelled for us to gather around, and he divided us into two teams for a practice game. I elbowed my way to the front of the group standing around our coach and looked him in the belt buckle. I was excited; finally a game, a chance to really play the game.

Then the coach asked the fateful question, "Who wants to pitch?" I'd been around enough baseball to know where the action was and who the star of the winning team would be.

Without a thought I shot my hand upward, yelling "I do! I do! I do!"

On about the second "I do," I realized I'd just poked my fingers into the coach's eye.

What a Letdown!

What followed wasn't pretty. Practice ended abruptly, with my coach making a quick trip to the emergency room. Instead of being the pitching star on the winning team, I was the goat at practice. I was the reason no one was playing, and I had nowhere to hide. I went home and never came back.

Often our lives brim with lofty dreams and expectations, but when we try to manipulate circumstances in our favor we create chaos and disappointment. With one desperate attention-seeking action, our dreams of heroism dissolve into "goathood."

The Scriptures can help us here. First Peter 5:6-7 says,

Humble yourselves, therefore, under God's mighty hand, that he may lift you up in due time. Cast all your anxiety on him because he cares for you.

Here we have at least three important lessons regarding a more humble approach to life. First, we can remember that God's mighty hand is almost always an image of His protection. We tend to think of God's hand as a powerful force to humble us (if we don't do the job ourselves). But His hand is primarily there to protect us when we assume the vulnerable position of humility. When we humble ourselves, we open our lives to the attacks of those who would like to use us as stepping stones for their own advancement. Thus when we humble ourselves, we demonstrate our dependence upon God's power to protect us.

He'll Pick You Up

Second, we can leave the exaltation of our lives to God alone. "That he may lift you up in due time" means just that. But His timing is key. Our goal should be to perform faithfully wherever God has placed us. There we can strive to learn all we can so we'll be prepared as God gives us greater authority and responsibility. We can relax in God's sovereign grace and be faithful to the tasks He has put before us.

Third, we can take the concerns about our career, accomplishment, finances, and family to God—and trust Him to do what is best. God loves us more than we love ourselves, and He knows everything about us. Why do we want to shoulder the burdens He has offered to carry?

We all want to be the pitcher. We all want the glory coming from some spotlight somewhere. Yet God says to wait for His timing and to carry on faithfully with the tasks He has given to us.

DAN BOLIN

EXTRA INNINGS
READ MATTHEW 23:11-12

- Can you think of a situation in which self-promotion actually hurt or hindered someone's career? What happened?
- Do you think the exaltation of the humble will occur primarily in this life or the next? Why?

NINETEEN

RELIEF PITCHER

ONE OF THE MORE SIGNIFICANT CHANGES IN BASEBALL OVER the past few decades has been the expanded role of the relief pitcher. Instead of guys waiting for a chance to show their stuff and becoming starting pitchers, the game has developed specialties for long relief, setup men, and closers. Of course, these come in both right- and left-handed varieties. It is normal for three, four, even five or more pitchers to throw in any ball game. A nine-inning performance from a starting pitcher is so rare that they now keep statistics on complete games.

Managers today realize the importance of keeping fresh arms throwing in the late innings. In the good old days, the starting pitcher threw and threw and often ended his career prematurely. Instead of thinking of relief pitchers only as a last resort, today's managers see them as a critical part of every game. Coaches study pitch counts and keep lifetime batting averages for every opposing batter against each of their pitchers.

Relief Is Available

We all need relief pitchers to come into the game for us from time to time. We pitch strong for a few innings and then we get hammered. Projects at work fall under criticism, our boss hollers, family relationships tense up, and the money can't cover the bills.

Something inside of us wants to keep pitching, though. Just like a big leaguer, we think that by trying a little harder or working a little longer we'll find the strength to turn things around. But in reality we just dig the hole deeper. Fortunately, Jesus Himself wants to be our relief pitcher. In Matthew 11:28-30 He says,

"Come to me, all you who are weary and burdened, and I will give you rest. Take my yoke upon you and learn from me, for I am gentle and humble in heart, and you will find rest for your souls. For my yoke is easy and my burden is light."

The first great truth in these verses is that Jesus wants us to come to Him with our burdens. I tend to think that I have to get my life in order before I will be *worthy* of His help and support. Nothing could be further from the truth. He says come when things are a mess, when the problems are insurmountable, when there appears to be no way out.

Another reason I keep striving when the burdens are unbearable is that I think I'll get in trouble for creating the problem. Most often a sinful act, stupid decision, or just plain negligence has created the problem in the first place, and I expect to be taken to the woodshed for it. What Jesus tells us is that His offer for relief comes from His gentle and humble heart. He won't kick us when we're down, nor will He turn His back on the brokenhearted. We may pay the consequences for our behavior, but His loving arms will always be ready to scoop us up and carry us through the darkest of times.

The third truth from this passage is that the learning process is at the heart of His compassionate care for us. Jesus says He wants us to learn from him. He wants us to break the patterns that got us into the mess in the first place. He wants us to develop patterns of dependence upon Him in the good times as well as in the periods of crisis. Then we should look for opportunities to be Christlike and lift burdens of those around us. While we are benefiting from Jesus' gentleness, we should be developing this quality ourselves.

The final lesson from these verses is that true rest only comes from Jesus. Rest doesn't mean we quit doing; it means that we strive to be faithful and rely on Him for the results. Rest comes as we are freed from carrying the burdens of life.

Don't let pride keep you from asking for heavenly relief. When the "hits" are pounding you, call for the relief that only God can provide.

DAN BOLIN

EXTRA INNINGS
READ 2 CORINTHIANS 12:7-10

- What area of weakness seems to plague you the most? How could you trust God for strength in this weakness?
- Who could you encourage today? How could you "be" God's source of strength for him or her?

*

TWENTY

TED WILLIAMS

TED WILLIAMS IS SAID TO HAVE BEEN THE BEST HITTER IN the history of baseball. Ted Williams is also said to have been a better fisherman than he was a hitter.

Back in the days when major league ball players had to work in the off-season to support their families, Ted sold fishing tackle. He made appointments and went from home to home peddling his wares. I know this, because my friend Bill told me.

Something to Talk About
One winter day, when Bill was about twelve years old, he received an excited phone call from his friend Eddie. "Hey, Bill! Can you come over right away? Ted Williams is in the house across the street. I saw him with my own eyes!"

Bill hopped on his bike and pedaled the mile and a half to Eddie's house as fast as his legs could get him there. After collaborating for a few minutes, the boys decided on a bold maneuver. They would walk across the street, knock on the door, and take a chance at being invited in. They figured this was their best shot at seeing their hero in person, and perhaps they would even get a chance to talk about baseball with him.

Sure enough, the kindly neighbor invited them in. As they entered the living room, there sat Ted Williams on the sofa surrounded by fishing tackle. Slowly he unfolded his large, lanky frame and stood to greet the boys. Slowly he shook their hands. He asked how they were doing and if they happened to play baseball. They replied that they did, and somewhere in the course of the introductions, Bill mentioned that he really liked to hit. This struck a chord with Ted, and thus began a thirty-minute conversation about the game of baseball. The famous major leaguer even asked Bill to demonstrate his batting style and then proceeded to unveil some of his own secrets to hitting.

Nothing Like Personal Access

His few minutes in the presence of Ted Williams became one of the most memorable experiences of Bill's childhood. From time to time he would read maligning articles about his idol circulated by the Boston press, but he never believed a single one because of his personal experience with the greatest hitter of all time. Bill's personal access to Ted Williams produced a life-changing moment in time.

Personal access is also a great part of our spiritual lives. Hebrews 4:16 says,

> *Let us therefore draw near with confidence to the throne of grace, that we may receive mercy and find grace to help in time of need.*

We have access to the very throne room of God! We are invited to enter boldly into the presence of the King of the Universe. How can this be possible?

Earlier in Hebrews 4 the writer tells us that "we have a great high priest who has passed through the heavens—Jesus the Son of God." You see, we do not deserve admission into God's presence any more than two twelve-year-old boys deserved an audience with Ted Williams. It's only because we have a "great high priest" that we are allowed to "draw near" to God. Jesus, our great high priest, has provided us with this access, just as Eddie's neighbor provided the boys with access to Mr. Williams.

Our high priest has done more for us than we can ever comprehend. He knows we are unable to enter the throne room of God on our own. To put it into baseball terminology, God only allows "perfect hitters" into His presence. Jesus is the only one who ever maintained a batting average of 1.000 in terms of righteous behavior. He never failed—not one single time. Yet, verse 15 of Hebrews 4 tells us,

We do not have a high priest who cannot sympathize with our weaknesses, but one who has been tempted in all things as we are, yet without sin.

Christ understands our weaknesses and the temptations we face. He actually experienced them just as we do, "yet without sin." But it is only because Christ Jesus bestows upon us His perfect batting average that we are admitted into God's presence. With a 1.000 average conferred upon us, we now can "draw near with confidence to the throne of grace."

Jesus, our high priest, built a bridge from us to our perfect heavenly Father. In fact, the Latin word for *priest* is *pontifax*—literally "bridge builder." What a shame it would be to waste Christ's sacrifice and His gift by not stepping boldly into the throne room of God to experience His mercy and grace!

In later years, Bill went on to play second base on his high school team. He was a good player, but he never became a great hitter. Bill would have given almost anything to have the great Ted Williams' Hall of Fame batting average conferred upon him. How much more should we desire to have the perfect life and sacrifice of Jesus be our very own in the eyes of God!

ED DIAZ

EXTRA INNINGS
READ ROMANS 5:1-5

- How can we have peace with God and access into His presence?
- How might you put this knowledge to use in your daily life?

TWENTY-ONE

A-2000

I'D COVETED THE WILSON A-2000 FOR YEARS. I FINALLY GOT the glove second-hand, but this was the real deal: fine leather, deep pocket, great fit. I was thrilled. I'd played with hand-me-downs and off-brand gloves for my first few years of Little League, but when I got my A-2000 I knew I was in the big time.

An Erroneous Conception
I was under the mistaken impression, however, that the glove made the player. No doubt the glove helps the player, and it would be impossible to play anything resembling modern baseball without a good glove. But in reality the ball player makes the glove. No matter how well-crafted the glove, it's only as good as the hand that goes inside. The hand of Brooks Robinson or Cal Ripkin makes the glove an all-star.

Without the master's hand the glove can do nothing. This doesn't disparage the worth of a glove that was created to accomplish a specific purpose. But the mitt has limited ability and capacity. Without the power of its owner, a baseball glove cannot accomplish the tasks it was designed to do.

An Essential Connection
The Christian life has two truths that are similar to the truth

of the glove. The first is found in Jesus' words in John 15:5 when He said,

"Apart from me you can do nothing."

Most of us take it for granted that we can walk and talk, eat and sleep, and live life pretty much on our own. In reality, every breath we take, every word we utter—our entire existence—depends upon God's gracious provision.

The inner circle of Christ's closest followers—the disciples—received this statement. If any group could have pleased God on its own it should have been Peter, James, John, and the rest of the disciples who had seen Jesus perform miracles and listened to Him teach. But Jesus says that none of us can accomplish anything for God unless we are connected to Him.

We may appear productive and even help others through our efforts, but there is no eternal value unless we stay connected to the Vine. When the glove comes off, it is on its own and has little hope of accomplishing what it was designed for. So we Christians have no hope of accomplishing the things we were designed for if we lose connection with Christ.

We must always see ourselves as the glove with God's power and skill providing all we need to be effective. We do not become mindless, heartless robots, because God uses our unique talents and experiences to His best advantage.

The second truth that applies to the baseball-glove image comes to us in Philippians 4:13,

I can do everything through him who gives me strength.

Just as we are limited without God's hand of power in our

lives, the opportunities are limitless when we trust Him to use us. With God's limitless power surging through us, we have the ability to do great things for Him. That may include doing a special project for God, but it may be that His power enables us to forgive someone who has hurt us deeply. Or His strength may allow us to endure a painful hardship with an acceptance that is beyond our natural capacity. Or we may be given the strength to teach a fourth grade boys' Sunday school class for one more week.

The two truths I've described are two sides of the same coin. *Without* God we can do nothing. *With* Him we have unlimited opportunity to accomplish His plan for our lives.

The challenge is to keep His hand connected to our lives, to remain constantly aware of His indwelling presence. His provision is powerful and He is always willing to supply the strength this life requires.

DAN BOLIN

EXTRA INNINGS
READ MATTHEW 28:18-20

- Why do you think Jesus told the disciples about His authority in verse 18?
- How do you think the disciples felt when Jesus told them He would be with them always?
- To what extent are you certain that Christ is always with you, even in the toughest times?

TWENTY-TWO

THE ALL-STAR GAME

SEVERAL YEARS OF LITTLE LEAGUE CAME DOWN TO THIS: Would I make the all-stars, or not? We all knew our team would win its way to Williamsport and be crowned champions of the world.

But would I be on that team?

I was a wreck as I waited for the coach's meeting deciding which of us would receive a coveted spot on the roster. I wasn't all that bad a player, but I wasn't great either.

Then came Coach's phone call: "Dan, you haven't been put on the team roster—yet. You're the first alternate; you could be on the team if somebody gets hurt or has to drop out. So keep your schedule open for a few days."

Mixed emotions, for sure! But a few days later I got another call: "Chuck's family vacation couldn't be changed. Can you be at practice this afternoon?"

Trading Places

Chuck's loss was my gain. With him giving up what was rightfully his, I had the opportunity to join a very special team.

Substitution offers a crucial opportunity in Christianity, too. The Christian life is somewhat like Chuck taking a painful position, and my joy at joining the all-star team. In 2 Corinthians 5:21 we read,

> *God made him who had no sin to be sin for us, so that in him we might become the righteousness of God.*

It cost Jesus everything to put us on God's all-star team. Books have been written, sermons preached, and classes taught to address the deep truth contained within this sentence of verse 21. But for our purposes, let's just focus on two basic truths. First, our substitute was perfect. No sin ever got a foothold in Jesus' life. He never disobeyed, told a lie, or acted out of pride or lust. Only a perfectly sinless substitute would qualify to take our place and absorb the punishing blows intended for us.

Second, not only did He take away our sin but He also provided us with God's righteousness. This is amazing! He didn't just remove the evil in our lives; He also filled us with the righteousness of God. Removing our sin would be great by itself, but to take our empty lives and fill them with a storehouse of goodness that we don't deserve is mind-boggling. Titus 2:14 picks up the same theme,

> *[He] gave himself for us, to redeem us from all wickedness and to purify for himself a people that are his very own, eager to do what is good.*

Living Gratefully

Consider two more of the most wonderful truths here. First, God desires a people of His very own. He wants a group of those who are deeply in love with Him, bonded with Him in a deep, committed relationship. God designed us for a relationship with Him, and He substituted Himself for us so we could enjoy this restored relationship. What more could we do than say thank you with a life of love and service?

And that brings us to the second wonderful truth, which has to do with our response to all God has done for us: We are to be *eager* to do what is good. Christianity isn't just another religion that puts us on a grueling treadmill of works so we can make a desperate attempt to please God and win His favor. No, His favor is unconditional. We do not do good deeds to *earn* God's acceptance; rather, we do good deeds because we already have His acceptance. Our works simply flow from gratitude.

Without His gracious substitution we would have been left off God's all-star team altogether. But He traded places with us, and that has made all the difference. He took away our sin and filled our lives with His righteousness. He made us part of a special group that He loves passionately. And we, in turn, should desire to work hard to please Him as the best players we can be.

Dan Bolin

EXTRA INNINGS
READ GENESIS 22:1-14

- What symbolism does this story hold for you?
- Do you have any insights into God the Father's heart as you sense the struggle in Abraham's life?

TWENTY THREE

CASEY AT THE BAT

ERNEST THAYER'S CLASSIC POEM "CASEY AT THE BAT" CAPTURES the intense emotion and formidable challenge of baseball (and of life). I'm sure you recall the gist of it: Opportunity presents itself to mighty Casey, the power-hitting superstar, when Flynn and Blake get on base during a two-out rally in the bottom of the ninth. Casey, the hometown favorite, gets his chance to hit the game winning home run. But he also gets a chance to be the goat.

The two-out, two-strike pitch speeds toward a mighty swing. But instead of sending the ball over the fence, Casey merely generates a prodigious whoosh of air—a sudden, stunning failure. And the Mudville Nine go down in defeat.

As a kid, I loved hearing my grandfather recite the poem at the dinner table. One part always intrigued me:

A straggling few got up to go.
    In deep despair the rest
clung to that hope which springs eternal
    in the human breast.

Hope On!

Hope is a part of our humanity. We want things to turn out all right. We want to win, to have happy endings, and to live happily ever after. Hope in this sense is more like a wish. We desire something that may or may not be reality. We long for things to work out for the best.

However, Scripture uses the word *hope* in a different way. Hope isn't a mere wish but an unseen reality. It's a rock-solid, done-deal that gives us strength to weather the storms of this life. Hebrews 6:19 puts it this way:

We have this hope as an anchor for the soul, firm and secure.

This hope is much more than a wish that God may be there and that He may have some small interest in our lives and destiny. Rather, it's a hope tethered to the character of God Himself and the truth of His Word. Because the Christian's hope rests on these immovable objects it becomes a secure anchor during the storms of life. Life's storms will howl and they will blow at us unexpectedly. That is when we need more than a wish. We need hope that is rock solid, firm, and secure for our souls.

Yet we must be careful what we expect and declare as promises from God. Too often I hear claims about promises recorded in Scripture but directed to another time and another place. Ultimately, our hope is not that events will work out in our favor; instead, our hope is that God will *use the events of our lives to make us more like His Son.* The writer of Hebrews goes on to say (in 10:23),

Let us hold unswervingly to the hope we profess, for he who promised is faithful.

Hang On!

Unlike a wish that we cling to, not knowing if it can be trusted, our hope as Christians is unmovable. The promise is firm, but we need to hang on tight. The writer calls us to hold on unswervingly. No matter what storms blast against us, hope is there if we hold on.

Our hope for forgiveness of sin, our hope for God's grace to be poured out in our lives, our hope for our eternal destiny to be fulfilled—all are to be grasped without hesitation. And all of these things are much more than a wish; they are the unseen realities of our existence.

Though we must keep hanging on, the true glory of hope comes down to the Giver of hope. That's because the reality we hope for is only as good as the one who made the promise to us. If a liar promises us a gift, we will probably never see it. But God's character is to be faithful. When God makes a promise He will live up to His end of the bargain. And, unlike Casey, we will hit that winning run.

DAN BOLIN

EXTRA INNINGS
READ PSALM 33:17-18

- What kinds of "false hope" are you most tempted to trust these days?
- What is the relationship between our hope and God's love? How does this relationship play out in your life?

TWENTY-FOUR

OLD-TIMER'S GAME

Twice I've had the pleasure of playing in a fund-raising event with some of the legends of the game. What a thrill to face Catfish Hunter and take him deep (behind the mound with a pop-up)! What joy to sit next to Cliff Johnson and Maury Wills in the dugout and be coached by Lou Burdett! These were real fantasy games. Across the field I saw the likes of Gaylord Perry, Ferguson Jenkins, Toby Harrah, and Jim Sundberg.

Pete O'Brien was our team's starting first baseman, and I was to come off the bench to play first later in the game. But just before the game's opening pitch, the local evening news decided to do a live interview with Pete in the right-field corner. I was summoned from the dugout to fill in for Pete until the interview concluded so as not to keep the fans sweltering any longer than necessary in the Tyler, Texas, heat.

The first pitch was missed, and I looked over my shoulder hoping that Pete would return before anything was hit in my direction. The interview was wrapping up, and he was heading my way, but there would be one more pitch, which became a grounder to short.

I covered the bag, ready for the ball, but the throw was up the line, flying past me into right-field foul territory. The runner rounded first and took off toward second as the ball rolled toward

O'Brien. He picked it up and threw a dart to second for the putout.

Nothing like an old-timer's game for bending the rules. Pete got the assist, and I got to return to the dugout while the crowd was still laughing.

Close to Perfect . . .

Being around some of the legends of the game is very revealing. On one hand, they're just like you and me. On the other, they're bigger than life, having reached an athletic pinnacle that brushes up against perfection.

In the Bible, Hebrews 11 is a chapter about the heroes of faith. It includes stories of people who did great things for God and overcame great hardship to serve Him. The amazing thing is that these people are just like us. Each of the people listed did great things for God but each had struggles along the way. Murderers, prostitutes, liars, cheaters, and drunkards all made the list.

Of course, this list doesn't condone behavior outside of God's directives for our lives, but it does give us hope. Romans 7:24-25 and 8:1 say,

> *What a wretched man I am! Who will rescue me from this body of death? Thanks be to God—through Jesus Christ our Lord. . . .Therefore, there is now no condemnation for those who are in Christ Jesus.*

. . . But Just Forgiven

When we look deeply at our sinful lives, we see wretchedness and failure. All too often our attempts to live godly lives come crashing down in defeat. We want victory over sin, but we fall short in our own power. And we'd be doomed to continual failure if it weren't for God's provision through Jesus. I'm sure Paul remembers his own sin and rebellion toward God when he exclaims, "Thanks be to God!" as he contemplates His forgiveness and right-standing before God through Jesus Christ.

Nevertheless, we are reminded of our sin, time and time again. We know God has forgiven us, but so often we can't seem to forgive ourselves. Satan loves to torment us by dredging up the past with all of its painful memories. That's why Paul keeps reminding us that the condemnation is gone if we are in Christ.

Yes, the heroes of Hebrews 11 all had their highlight films . . . and their bloopers, too. They were just like us. But when they fell down, they got up and went on. They forged ahead with a renewed desire to please God, with a deeper sense of God's grace, and with an awareness that God's heroes are not perfect, just forgiven.

DAN BOLIN

EXTRA INNINGS
READ PSALM 32:1-7

- In the psalmist's life, what was the result of keeping silent by not confessing his sin to God?
- What are the descriptions of the man who is blessed? How do you personally measure up to this description?

TWENTY-FIVE

THE LONGEST CRY BY A SHORTSTOP

MORE THAN ANY OTHER SPORT, BASEBALL IS KNOWN FOR keeping statistics. Everything is recorded, from the sublime to the ridiculous. If you're a fan, you know all the legendary stats: that Roger Maris held the single-season record for home runs (61 in 1961) for almost four decades, before Mark McGwire came along; or that "the iron horse" Lou Gehrig held the record for most consecutive games played, until Cal Ripken, Jr., finally surpassed him.

But are you are aware that the last person to hit .400 was Ted Williams (.407 in 1941)? Did you know that the Baltimore Orioles beat the New York Yankees 13 to 9, completing the longest nine-inning game ever played (4 hours and 22 minutes on September 5, 1997)? Or that only a record-low ninety-five fans showed up for a Boston Braves game on July 28, 1935?

What a Time Record!

Here's one record I'm sure you don't know: the longest cry by a shortstop. That record was set in 1985 by my son Ben. Ben was playing T-ball at the time, enjoying himself quite thoroughly. Since the coach allowed all the players equal playing time, he'd developed a routine in which every player sat on the bench for two innings. Ben was scheduled to sit out the third and fourth innings of every game. However, one evening, as the third inning rolled around, Ben's team was one player short. The coach immediately signaled for Ben to head out to cover the shortstop position.

As he obediently picked up his glove and jogged out to the field, tears started trickling down his face. He started sniffling, and before long he was crying—just standing there at shortstop holding his glove and crying. It wasn't a little wimpy cry, either. He cried loud and long.

No one could figure out what was wrong. Ben normally loved to play shortstop. A quick time-out didn't reveal any problem, so he stayed in the game. He cried so long that an entire inning passed him by. No one has ever challenged the fact that Ben Diaz holds the record for the longest cry by a shortstop.

When the inning ended, Ben stopped crying immediately. I corralled him and asked him what on earth had him so upset. His answer was simple: "I missed my turn on the bench. I like when it's my turn to be in the dugout, because we have fun in there."

A Time to Prepare

Being in the dugout is a part of baseball, but it's not usually all that fun. Every player, including the superstar, has to spend some time riding the pine. Sometimes it's just for a few minutes each inning while teammates are taking their turns at bat. Sometimes it's for a substitute to be sent into the game. Sometimes it's because the player in the dugout is only used in a specialty role. Whatever it's for, time spent in the dugout is always valuable time for recouping, observing, and learning.

The "dugout experience" is a very real part of our spiritual lives, as well. From time to time God sits each of us on the bench. Sometimes it's to give us much needed time to rest and reflect. Sometimes it's to take us away from a situation that could be harmful. Sometimes it's necessary time for the ones we are called to minister to—while their hearts are being prepared. Always it is a time God uses to teach and equip us. While we're riding the pine we can learn things we'd be too busy to absorb if we were caught up in playing the game itself.

Most of God's great servants spent time on the bench: Moses spent forty years in the dugout, learning to become a shepherd before he could lead the sheep of Israel from bondage to freedom. The apostle Paul spent more than thirteen years after his conversion sitting in the dugout, waiting until the church was ready to accept his special ability to minister to the Gentiles. And Jesus Himself spent forty days in the wilderness as He prepared for His public ministry here on earth.

Our Times: In His Hands

The dugout experience is different for each of us. It can come in the form of an illness that keeps us flat on our backs; by looking up we are forced to look at God. It can be a frustrating job experience where we feel we're not being used to our full potential, yet we are forced to learn about God's peace and contentment. Sometimes it's a personal relationship that is difficult, but God is using what seems like wasted time to prepare our heart so we can really hear what our friend is saying.

King David spent a lot of time sitting on the bench before he sat on the throne. It was often very difficult time spent fighting for his life or hiding in caves. Yet, he says,

> *But as for me, I trust in Thee, O LORD; I say, "Thou art my God." My times are in Thy hand.* (Psalm 31:14-15)

Sometimes it's hard to remember that God is the perfect coach. He knows when it's best to take us out of the ball game and when it's best to put us back in. Are you willing to trust God during the "dugout" times of your life? Can you, like David, let your daily schedule rest in God's hands?

ED DIAZ

EXTRA INNINGS
READ PSALM 78:70-72

- Read about David's "dugout experience." How did David's time in the sheep pens prepare him for his time of leadership?
- Has God placed you in the "dugout" lately? What was/is He teaching or preparing you for?

TWENTY-SIX

DODGER BLUES

TOMMY LASORDA, FORMER MANAGER OF THE LOS ANGELES Dodgers, tells one of my favorite baseball anecdotes. In the early eighties Dodger second baseman Steve Sax, for some unexplainable reason, had developed a "mental block" about throwing runners out at first base. Although the Dodgers tried everything from threats to hypnosis, Sax's problem grew worse. He simply could not throw the ball to first base accurately. Balls went in the dirt and over the fence—everywhere but where they were intended to go.

At the same time, Lasorda was experimenting with a player position change as well. Pedro Guererro had played the outfield during most of his major league career. The Dodgers had a surplus of outfielders but desperately needed a third baseman. Guererro was asked to try out for the spot, but the experiment was not going smoothly.

One day during pre-game practice, Lasorda decided he would help Guererro battle the mental aspects of playing third base. "Pete," he inquired. "What are you thinking as the pitcher goes into his wind-up?"

"That's easy," replied Guererro. "I'm thinking, 'Please don't hit it to me!'"

"Okay Pete," chuckled Lasorda. "But after you get that out of your mind, what's the *second* thing you're thinking?"

"I'm praying they don't hit it to Sax!"

It Happens at All Levels

Lest you think mental difficulties arise only at the major league level, let me assure you that similar problems occur with high school players. This past spring my high school team had a position surplus as well. Our dilemma was an abundance of infielders and too few outfielders. Hoping to solve our problem, we asked Carson (normally a third baseman) to play center field. Carson worked diligently to become an adequate outfielder. But practice and drills could not prepare him for real-game experience.

That happened during the first weekend of our season. One of my coaching duties is to "position" our defense. This can be done verbally with the infielders. However, since the outfielders are usually out of vocal range, a series of hand signals is necessary. After every batter, the outfield is to check with me and see if I want them to move in one direction or another before the next batter steps into the box. Carson simply couldn't remember to do this, and I found myself routinely hollering in his direction.

During a pitching change, I tried unsuccessfully to reach my rookie center fielder. Over and over I shouted, "Carson! . . . Carson! . . . Carson!" But Carson kept looking down, kicking at the stubble in the outfield grass. Finally, in great frustration, I yelled, "Carson! Look up!"

He did. He looked straight up toward heaven! The dugout

guys collapsed in laughter. But when Carson came in at the end of the inning he looked puzzled. "Coach, I looked up. But all I could see up there were birds."

It's the Ultimate "Mind Game"

Baseball is played between the ears more than any other sport. On every pitch, every player has to anticipate his responsibilities based on where the runners are, figuring out where the cut-off man should be, knowing where the back-up man has to go . . . and on and on. At every level of baseball beyond Little League, ability alone is not enough to play the game. All of the players are greatly talented. All can throw, hit, run, and catch with their peers. However, the big difference between the good players and the average players is the ability to anticipate mentally. A player unable to handle the mental part of the game cannot succeed.

Mental preparation is also a major part of the Christian life. *What* we believe ultimately determines *how* we behave. What we put into our minds determines our actions. The Scriptures often reinforce this truth. Philippians 4:8 says,

> *Finally, brethren, whatever is true, whatever is honorable, whatever is right, whatever is pure, whatever is lovely, whatever is of good repute, if there is any excellence and if anything worthy of praise, let your mind dwell on these things.*

The apostle Paul understood the importance of mental preparation. If we spend all our waking moments with our minds on worldly affairs, it's likely that when we face a spiritual dilemma we'll respond in a worldly way. Paul goes on in Philippians 4:9 to say,

The things you have learned and received and heard and seen in me, practice these things; and the God of peace shall be with you.

Paul emphasizes that training the mind (verse 8) should come before practicing our faith (verse 9). The incredible result is that "the God of peace shall be with you." Often we fail to enjoy God's peace because we have not focused our minds on those things that are true, honorable, right, and pure.

When Pedro Guererro first tried to play third base, he had no peace at all. His mind swirled with doubts and anxieties about what might occur. And when we fail to train our minds to focus on the things that will please God, we too will find ourselves frustrated, anxious, and full of doubts each day.

I know it's the case with me. How about you? What is your mind dwelling on these days?

ED DIAZ

EXTRA INNINGS
READ PSALM 139:1-4

- In what ways are you *comforted* today by knowing God is fully aware of everything your mind dwells on?
- In what ways are you *convicted* by knowing God is fully aware of everything your mind dwells on?
- Read verses 23 and 24 at the end of the psalm. Will you pray that prayer with the psalmist right now?

FENCES: FRIEND OR FOE?

As the youngest of four brothers, Jonathan grew up in a hurry. He always tried to emulate his older siblings in every way. Therefore, ever since he was a toddler, he has hung out at the ball field. He seldom got in their way as a youngster, and his brothers found him particularly useful if they needed help shagging balls during batting practice. All he required in return was a couple of turns at the plate and several opportunities to race around the base paths.

However, by age eleven, Jonathan felt he could and should do *everything* his older brothers did. He took his turn at bat just like they did, practiced infield with them, fielded grounders for them, and chased down fly balls in the outfield.

The one thing Jonathan was not allowed to do, however, was drive the golf cart.

I Don't Like 'Em!

"What was a golf cart doing at the baseball field?" you ask.

The golf cart had been purchased for Coach Carpenter, head coach of the high school team, who suffers with rheumatoid arthritis. But my sons had found that when Coach Carpenter wasn't using it, the "buggy" could be very helpful in shagging batting practice balls. So, one by one, each batter would hit an entire bucket of baseballs. Then a few players would jump aboard the buggy and traverse the outfield dutifully picking up stray balls.

Jonathan's job in those days was to chase any balls that went beyond the fence—both fair and foul. On one particular occasion, however, he was bold enough to ask if he might drive the buggy while his brothers took a water break. Coach Carpenter responded, "Sure, you can drive the buggy. I don't suppose there's anything out there you can run into—except maybe the fence." He chuckled at his own somewhat sarcastic statement.

Well, you guessed it. Within a few minutes, while trying to scoop up a ball that had traveled the full extent of the field, Jonathan ran the golf cart right into the fence. At first, we thought it was funny. Unfortunately, in trying to push away from the fence with his left foot, Jonathan got his toes stuck in the chain link. The cart kept rolling, pulling him along with it—twisting and breaking his left leg in three places!

As we loaded Jonathan from the buggy into the back seat of our car, he muttered, "Why did they have to put a fence there? I really don't like fences."

Why the Fences?

There are times in my life when I'm tempted to cling to that same sentiment—I really don't like fences either. It seems as though God often puts boundaries in our lives, daunting barriers that are quite inconvenient or painful. Why does He do this? James 1:23-25 says,

If any one is a hearer of the word and not a doer, he is like a man who looks at his natural face in a mirror; for once he has looked at himself and gone away, he has immediately forgotten what kind of person he was. But one who looks intently at the perfect law, the law of liberty, and abides by it, not having become a forgetful hearer but an effectual doer, this man shall be blessed in what he does.

Verse 25 contains an interesting concept, especially when it comes to our view of the fences or boundaries that God erects around us. James calls God's perfect law the "law of liberty." At first glance the phrase "law of liberty" seems to be an oxymoron. Aren't "laws" the opposite of "liberty"? However, as we look closely, it begins to make sense. The law of liberty is the fence God establishes that actually *allows us the freedom to do what He desires.*

This One's Okay!

The game of baseball has all sorts of boundaries and rules—"laws" if you will. The fence acts as a boundary between a ball in play and one out of play. Foul lines clearly denote the playing area. Foul poles (sometimes called "fair poles") determine whether a batted ball is a home run or merely a long strike.

These boundaries set us free to play the game. Without boundaries, baseball as we know it would be impossible. Suppose you were allowed to run around the bases in any direction or in any order? Suppose any batted ball could be played as fair? Baseball as a sport would cease to exist. Therefore, these rules set us free to play the game as it was intended.

In the same way, God's law sets us free to become the men that He intends us to become. We are to diligently study His law—not like a man "who looks at his natural face in a mirror." Rather we are to "look intently at the perfect law"—and obey it—in order to experience God's blessing.

After three months in a cast, Jonathan's leg healed, and his Little League all-star team made it to the finals. At a critical time, Jonathan knocked a home run over a fence that was much closer than the one he was used to hitting at. As he circled third base he happily muttered to himself, "I like that fence."

ED DIAZ

EXTRA INNINGS
READ PSALM 19:7-11

- What "liberties" do God's laws provide?
- Think of a time that you chose to obey one of God's laws rather than step outside His boundaries. What liberty did that obedience produce in your life?

TWENTY-EIGHT

HENRY AARON

MOST BASEBALL FANS KNOW THAT HANK AARON HOLDS THE lifetime record for home runs: 755. But many fans aren't aware that Aaron never saw any of his major league homers actually leave the ballpark. This is because he was concentrating on touching first base instead of watching the trajectory of his round-tripper.

It all began in 1952 when Hank began his professional career playing "C Ball" in Eau Claire, Wisconsin. Aaron recalls hitting his first home run and watching the ball sail out of the stadium. Inadvertently, he missed first base and was called out! From that day on, Hank decided that touching first base was more important than seeing the ball leave the yard. So home run after home run he practiced the basics. Home run after home run he made absolutely sure he stepped on each bag as he rounded the infield.

Don't Get Bored!
Touching first base may seem an insignificant detail in the big picture of playing baseball. However, the greatest home run hitter of all time missed out on the joy of his very first professional dinger because of his seemingly inconsequential oversight.

As coaches, we tell our high school players that "*one* mistake can cost you *one* out; which can cost you *one* run; which can cost you *one* ball game; which can cost you *one* state championship." At our level of play, winning the state championship is the ultimate goal. But winning doesn't just happen on the day of the game in the state tournament. No, winning a championship begins many months before that.

It all begins in the fall. It's during the fall that high school players can work on bat plane, stride length, and the other mechanics of hitting. During the fall they practice fielding grounders and catching fly balls. And during the fall they live in the weight room to gain additional throwing strength and foot speed. All of this is critical, even though baseball is played in the spring.

Motivating young players to continually work on the basics is probably the greatest challenge in coaching. Often a player will ask, "Coach, what are we going to do at practice today?"

We almost always answer, "Well, we're going to hit it, we're going to catch it, we're going to throw it, and we're going to run! Any other questions?" After they shake their heads, pick up their gear, and trudge out onto the field, we holler after them, "And don't get bored with this!"

You see, in the game of baseball there are really only these four basic elements—hitting, catching, throwing, and running. The average player often gets bored with these details and stops working on them.

Hank Aaron was not only the greatest home run hitter of all time. He was also a very hard worker who paid attention to the basic details of the game. Most fans are unaware of the hard work and mental discipline that went into every one of his 755 career home runs. All they were able to see was the end result.

Keep Working on the Basics

In the same way, the Christian life has some basic elements, skills we must practice over and over and over—without getting bored!

"God, what are we going to do in life today?" you might ask.

"Well," says God. "I want you to pray, I want you to read your Bible, I want you to enjoy Christian fellowship, and I want you to share your faith."

So we do—for a while. Then, mistakenly, we think we've mastered the skill, or we find ourselves bored with the basics. So we stop practicing. Years later, when we experience failure in our walk with God, we're tempted to ask, "Why?" The answer is simple: We weren't willing to put in the hard work necessary during the practice days in order to win the spiritual battle later on.

The book of Acts tells us that the new believers grew tremendously in their faith. Not only was their personal faith growing, so were the numbers in their churches. New converts joined them daily as they observed the lifestyles of these new Christians. Acts 2:42 says,

> *They devoted themselves to the apostles' teaching and to the fellowship, to the breaking of bread and to prayer.*

These were the basics, and the early believers practiced them over and over. Many youngsters start out their baseball careers as superstars in their age bracket. But very few stick with the basics long enough to make it into high school ball, let alone college or the big leagues. And only one player has hit 755 home runs.

How many Christians do you know over the age of sixty who are still dynamic in their Christian walk? Who still read their Bibles and pray with enthusiasm? Who fellowship with other Christians heartily? Who share their faith with sustained vigor?

We must continually practice the basics. Don't get bored with this!

ED DIAZ

EXTRA INNINGS
READ PSALM 119:9-11

- What steps have you taken this week to keep your Christian walk pure and dynamic?
- Evaluate your closest friendships. Do you fellowship with anyone who challenges you to grow in your Christian walk? Do you challenge others?

TWENTY-NINE

THE STOP AND SLOP

KEVIN SEITZER WAS ONE OF MY FAVORITE MAJOR LEAGUERS. He always played the game aggressively, winning Rookie of the Year honors during his first year in "the Show." What a treat it was to watch Kevin have an impact with his faith during his thirteen-year career. However, one spring day when his team, the Kansas City Royals, showed up in Lakeland, Florida, for an exhibition game, Kevin was forced to ask the question that erupts from all of us sooner or later: "Why me?"

How 'Bout Somebody Else?
One of Kevin's friends, Frank Tanana, had also reported to spring training that year. He, too, was in Lakeland, on that same spring day; however, he was dressed in a Detroit Tigers uniform.

After fifteen years in the big leagues, Frank found spring training somewhat boring. In order to alleviate the tedium, Frank would work during the off-season to develop a better pitch or in some way enhance his effectiveness on the mound. Each spring he would try to perfect the new technique against opposing batters. This year, in particular, was unique in the history of American League baseball. Over the winter, you see, Frank had developed a brand new pitch that became known as the "Stop and Slop."

Here's how it worked: Frank would begin his normal wind-up and step toward home plate, but then—and this is the funny part—in the middle of his motion he would stop, with his front foot planted and his arm cocked in throwing position. From that awkward stance, while a batter stood baffled in the box, Frank would lob what he called an "ephus pitch" in the direction of home plate. Frank had worked on this trick in the bullpen and even during batting practice, but the pitch had yet to be tested in a game situation. That would occur during the first visit of the Kansas City Royals to Lakeland, Florida, the spring training home of the Detroit Tigers.

In the first inning, during Seitzer's first at bat, on a 1-2 count, Frank unloaded the dreaded Stop and Slop. The whole ballpark came to a standstill as Frank stood, arm cocked, ready to deliver who-knows-what.

Poor Kevin! All he could do was wait along with the rest of us.

As Frank finally unleashed his new weapon, the ball sailed lazily, in a high looping arc, toward home plate. With two strikes, and the ball dropping toward the strike zone, Kevin simply had to swing—and he did. The ball rolled weakly to short, and Seitzer, shaking his head in frustration, took off for first base. Halfway down the line he looked toward the mound and pleaded with Frank, "Why *me*?"

How Will You Respond?

We all ask, "Why me?" from time to time. It's not unusual to question some event in our lives, especially if that event borders on tragedy. The Old Testament is full of such examples. The book of Job spends many chapters in dialogue over this great theological inquiry.

In the New Testament, James writes a short epistle, part of which deals with this very question. In James 1:2-4 we read:

Consider it all joy, my brethren, when you encounter various trials, knowing that the testing of your faith produces endurance. And let endurance have its perfect result, that you may be perfect and complete, lacking in nothing.

You see, James doesn't focus on the question *why* so much as the timing of *when*. It's not a matter of whether we will experience difficulties—it's more a question of how to respond *when* trials occur.

James is writing to believers encountering many obstacles to their faith that might cause them to ask, "Why me, God?" However, the greater question they should be asking is this: "When trials occur, how will I respond to them?"

James says the believer in Christ can rejoice (verse 2), knowing that the trials are not God's ultimate goal. Rather, tough times are intended to produce in us endurance (verse 3), so that we may become perfect (or mature) and complete, "lacking in nothing" (verse 4). This whole process is defined as "wisdom" (verse 5).

What trial are you struggling with today? Is it possible that God can use this situation to infuse the qualities of endurance, maturity, and completeness into your life? If so, you will develop wisdom.

It's certainly okay to ask, "Why me, God?" But having asked that question, if we still don't understand God's greater purpose, the next thing we should ask is, "Lord, will you please grant me the wisdom to see your perspective in the trials I'm now experiencing?"

Kevin Seitzer found himself out at first base—hopefully a better man for the experience. (In the end, Frank Tanana received a letter from the American League president banning the Stop and Slop forever. However, that didn't keep him from trying to find creative new ways to produce "trials" for hitters he would face in seasons to come!)

ED DIAZ

EXTRA INNINGS
READ MATTHEW 11:28-30

- What does Christ want us to do when life's trials become burdensome? How have you coped during those times?
- What kind of rest does God promise us? How do you know when you are resting in God's arms?

THIRTY

THE DANGER OF DISQUALIFICATION

WHEN THE DUST FINALLY SETTLED, WE HAD ADVANCED TO the Columbia Park Little League championship game.

My highly acclaimed team had three pitchers, and I was one of them. We'd all won our share of games, but I was the biggest kid and probably the most intimidating hurler of the three. So when a big game was on the line, the coach worked the rotation for me to start. And with only two games left, I pitched a win in the first one.

Now for game two, I expected to put on the catcher's gear. But when I arrived at the field, Coach gave me one of the two shiny-white game balls and said, "Bolin, warm up." It was a gutsy call, but the result was spectacular: another win—this time for the championship!

We yelled and threw our hats into the air, jumped around the infield like crazed monkeys and savored the incredible thrill of being Number One.

At least for a moment. . . .

Straying Off Course?

You see, their coach and the umpire were talking. Pretty intently. Something about me pitching too many innings without enough days of rest. Something about the league rules.

A protest was filed that same day.

Even though we appeared to have won, we had in fact played the game outside of the rules. The championship was given to the team we'd defeated, and we received none of the honor we had made such a great run for. When it counted most, we strayed off course and succumbed to disqualification.

In 1 Corinthians 9, Paul talks about straying from the goal of spiritual maturity, which is the longed for "championship," the ultimate desire of every Christian. Beginning in verse 24 he says,

Do you not know that in a race all the runners run, but only one gets the prize? . . . Therefore I do not run like a man running aimlessly; I do not fight like a man beating the air. No, I beat my body and make it my slave so that after I have preached to others, I myself will not be disqualified for the prize.

Paul is making three key points. First, the goal of racing is to win. The race of life is not primarily for entertainment or pleasure; it has its high points but is not designed to be merely a "fun run." Rather, the goal is to win the prize. Winning requires intensity and hard work. It means leaving good things behind and running life's race with all we have. The race is tough, but the prize makes all the effort worthwhile.

Paul's second point has to do with staying on course. If a sprinter runs out of his lane or if a marathoner fails to stay on the prescribed course, he'll be disqualified. The issue here is focus. Keeping the end in view will keep us on track. Running aimlessly will exhaust us as quickly as running with focus, but it will produce no good results in our lives or in the lives of those around us. Paul likens this to shadow boxing, beating the air. We flail around, thoroughly busy and energetic, producing nothing for our effort.

The final issue is discipline. The apostle disciplines everything in his life so that he will stay focused on the goal, not losing his way and stumbling into areas of busy unproductivity. This is hard work. It means saying "no" to good things, saying "no" to sin, and saying "yes" to the challenges hurtling toward us every day.

Don't Be Disqualified!

Earlier in 1 Corinthians (3:10-15), Paul had already established the fact that our deeds will be tested by fire, and the works based on disqualified efforts will surely burn. Yet those of gold, silver, or costly stones will remain as true works of righteousness. Paul wants his focused efforts to be the real thing. He fears disqualification more than anything else.

We must compete to win with focus and purpose. The goal is not to get to the end of life exhausted and weary from racing aimlessly between pointless events. No, the goal is to be effective in service for God, to stay on track, to win the prize He has in store for us.

DAN BOLIN

EXTRA INNINGS
READ JOHN 14:21-24

- What is the relationship between love and obedience?
- What are some practical ways your own obedience has demonstrated your love for God in the past?

CALLING IT LIKE IT IS

He had finally made it to "the Show."

Having grown up in Virginia, just across the river from Baltimore, Larry Sheets was a lifelong Orioles fan. So it was a tremendous thrill for him to sign with his favorite club in 1978 right out of high school. He labored hard in the minor leagues until September of 1984. Near the end of his sixth season, Larry got the call from the major league club.

His Umpire Calls It

Now his friends and family were there to enjoy his moment in the sun. In his first home game at old Memorial Stadium, forty thousand fans showed up to watch their team battle to stay in the pennant race. To several dozen fans, however, the pennant race wasn't nearly as important as the opportunity to see their friend and family member play with the heroes of his youth. Even Larry's high school coach was seated among his special supporters.

Larry's "cheerleaders" rose to their feet and hollered as Larry approached home plate for his first major league at bat in Memorial Stadium—and what an at bat it was! Larry worked the count to 2 and 1, then proceeded to foul off several pitches. He gained more fans, and the cheers grew louder with every pitch. After eight foul balls in a row, Larry took a pitch that was up and away. He threw his bat down and jogged to first base.

As he stood relieved on the bag and began to remove his batting gloves, the umpire approached him. "Son," he said. "I don't know what league you've been playing in—but it takes *four* balls to draw a walk up here!"

Sheepishly Larry trudged back to the plate amid the cheers and jeers of the fans, then dug in on a full count. The pitcher, thinking Larry had tried to show him up, threw the next pitch at his head. Larry picked himself up off the clay and *walked* to first base.

Larry's high school coach joked after the game, "I always figured they had to push you ahead each grade—you never could have graduated being that dumb!"

Your "Ump" Calls It, Too!

Yes, it takes four balls to walk in any league. And ultimately, which pitches are balls and which ones are strikes is determined by an umpire. As one old umpire once summarized it, "Some of 'em is balls—and some of 'em is strikes—but they ain't nothin' 'til I calls 'em!"

Indeed, umpires are a critical element in the game of baseball, but did you know that Scripture refers to umpires as well? In Job chapter 9, we find Job defending himself from the accusations of his friend Bildad. Since Job was plagued with suffering for no apparent reason, his friends tried hard to convince him that in some way he deserved his fate as punishment for wrongdoing. Job protested, declaring his innocence. He longed to go before God and argue his case; however, Job realized that would be impossible. In 9:32-33 we read Job's dilemma:

For He is not a man as I am that I may answer Him, that we may go to court together. There is no umpire between us who may lay his hand upon us both.

Job longed for an umpire—a mediator who would be both fair and faithful—to plead his case.

In Hebrews 5, we find that Jesus Christ is the fulfillment of Job's desire. He is our mediator, our umpire. He can be totally fair, because He understands our every need. In addition, Jesus Christ is an umpire who is completely faithful. After all, He offered the ultimate sacrifice for us. Through His death on the cross, we have the promise of forgiveness and God's guarantee of eternal life.

Every time we're involved in a "close play at the plate," we have an umpire who steps forward and declares, "You are safe at home." And since that's the way He calls it, that's the way it is.

ED DIAZ

EXTRA INNINGS
READ JOHN 17:11-26

- In Christ's prayer to His Father just before His death, He stands up for all believers. What are some of the things He requests on our behalf?
- In what ways will knowing that Christ is your faithful mediator help you finish this week?

ABOUT THE AUTHORS

DAN BOLIN is the president of Dan Bolin Resources, Inc., which provides ministry, marketing, management, and fundraising support to Christian nonprofit ministries. He is also a senior associate with the Goehner Resource Group and a regional representative for Christian Camping International.

Dan earned his bachelor's degree from Seattle Pacific University and his master's of theology degree from Dallas Theological Seminary. He also holds an MBA from LeTourneu University.

A frequent speaker both nationally and internationally, Dan is the author or coauthor of several books, including *A Hole in One, The One That Got Away, Avoiding the Blitz, How to Be Your Daughter's Daddy, How to Be Your Little Man's Dad,* and *How to Be Your Wife's Best Friend.* He has also been published in *Decision Magazine* and *The Journal of Christian Camping.*

Dan, his wife Cay, and their daughter Haley live near Tyler, Texas, where he serves as an elder at Bethel Bible Church and as a board member of Dan Anderson Ministries and the Tyler Independent School District.

ED DIAZ is a Southern Division Director for Search Ministries—a ministry of lifestyle evangelism to the business community. In addition, Ed has served as Spring Training chapel coordinator for the Detroit Tigers over the last 15 years. He regularly leads Bible studies for various professional teams. His love of baseball has been nurtured by coaching on the high school level.

Ed helped to start Walk Thru the Bible Ministries, and he has taught their seminars since 1974. Ed and his family reside in Lakeland, Florida.

If you liked THE WINNING RUN, you'll love these other books by Dan Bolin.

A Hole in One

Is the draw of the golf green interfering with your time with God? Combine your time with Him with your interest in golf to discover His perspectives on life and deepen your relationship with Him.

A Hole in One
(Dan Bolin) $10

Avoiding the Blitz

Gain yardage on the field of life with this devotional. Discover how your love of football can help you apply a spiritual truth and lesson for life in under ten minutes each day!

Avoiding the Blitz
(Dan Bolin) $10

The One That Got Away

Designed for under ten minutes of daily reading, each section of this "catchy" devotional highlights an element of fishing. Apply a spiritual truth and lesson for your life through interesting stories about your favorite sport.

The One That Got Away
(Dan Bolin) $10

Get your copies today at your local bookstore, through our website, or by calling (800) 366-7788.
(Ask for offer **#2343** or a FREE catalog of NavPress products.)

NAVPRESS
BRINGING TRUTH TO LIFE
www.navpress.com

Prices subject to change.